HAPPINESS

The Only True
Prosperity

OSHO

INSIGHTS FOR A
NEW WAY OF LIVING

ST. MARTIN'S
ESSENTIALS
NEW YORK

Published in the United States by St. Martin's Essentials,
an imprint of St. Martin's Publishing Group

The material in this book is selected from various talks by Osho given to a live audience.
All of Osho's talks have been published in full as books and are also available as original
audio recordings. Audio recordings and the complete text archive can be found via the
online OSHO Library at www.osho.com.

OSHO® is a registered trademark of Osho International Foundation,
www.osho.com/trademarks.

www.stmartins.com

Library of Congress Cataloging-in-Publication Data

Names: Osho, 1931–1990, author.
Title: Happiness: The Only True Prosperity / Osho.
Description: First St. Martin's Essentials. | New York, NY : St. Martin's
    Essentials [2023] | Series: Osho Iinsights for a New Way of Living
Identifiers: LCCN 2022020117 | ISBN 9781250786326 (trade paperback) |
    ISBN 9781250786333 (ebook)
Subjects: LCSH: Happiness—Religious aspects. | Joy—Religious aspects.
Classification: LCC BP605.R34 H35 2023 | DDC 299/.93—dc23/eng/20220621
LC record available at https://lccn.loc.gov/2022020117

Our books may be purchased in bulk for promotional, educational, or business use.
Please contact your local bookseller or the Macmillan Corporate and
Premium Sales Department at 1-800-221-7945, extension 5442, or
by email at MacmillanSpecialMarkets@macmillan.com.

First St. Martin's Essentials Edition: 2023

10 9 8 7 6 5 4 3 2 1

Also by Osho

Contents

Contents

Introduction

would like to know whether you are satisfied with material things or whether you want to develop your consciousness. One who is satisfied with the outside world will always be basically unhappy. This kind of life is simply one of convenience. Convenience is only the absence of trouble, whereas real satisfaction is the attainment of happiness.

What does your heart say? What is the greatest desire of your life? Have you ever asked yourself these questions? If not, then let me ask you now. If you were to ask me, I would reply that I wish to attain that state where nothing further remains to be attained. Is this not the answer that pulsates in your innermost soul as well? I do not ask this question of you alone; I have also asked it of thousands and thousands of others.

It is my observation that all human hearts are the same and that their ultimate desire is also the same. This soul wants happiness, perfect and pure happiness, because only then will all desires end.

As long as desire exists, misery exists, because with desire there can be no peace.

The total absence of desire brings happiness. It also brings freedom and liberation, because whenever something is lacking, there are both limits and dependency. Only when nothing at all is lacking is there the possibility of total freedom. Freedom brings happiness. And happiness is salvation.

The desire for total happiness and for ultimate freedom lies dormant in everyone. It is in the form of a seed. It is like a seed that contains a tree within it. In the same way, the fulfillment of man's ultimate desire is hidden in his very nature. In its perfectly developed state, it is our nature to be happy, to be free. Our real nature is the only thing that is true, and only perfecting it can bring complete satisfaction.

The one who does not seek to fulfill his own nature mistakenly thinks prosperity will alleviate his misery. But material wealth can never fill his inner emptiness. And so, even when a person attains everything possible in the world, he still feels that he has missed out on something. His innermost being remains empty. As Buddha once said, "Desire is difficult to fulfill."

It is strange that no matter what a person may attain, he is never satisfied—that even after he has accomplished his goal, he yearns for still greater achievements. And so the poverty of beggars and emperors is the same. At this level, there is no difference between them at all.

No matter what gains a person makes in the outer world, they are unstable. They can be lost, destroyed at any time, and in the end death claims them. So it is not surprising that one's inner heart is never fulfilled by these sorts of things, by things that can so easily be taken away. This kind of prosperity will never give a person a sense of security, no matter how strenuously he pursues it. What really happens is that now he has to provide security for the things he has acquired.

It must be clearly understood that outward power and prosperity can never eradicate one's sense of want, one's insecurity, or one's fear. Self-deception is the only way to camouflage these feelings. Prosperity is an intoxicant; it hides the reality of life. And this type of forgetfulness is far worse than poverty itself because it prevents you from doing anything to rid yourself of your real poverty. Real poverty is not caused by the absence of any material object nor by the lack of power or prosperity, because even if one becomes rich and powerful, it is still there. Do you not see the poverty of those who seem to have everything? Have your burdens ever been lightened by your material possessions?

My friends, there is a great difference between prosperity and the illusion of prosperity. All external wealth, power, and security are but shadows of the real riches that exist within you. The basic reason for this feeling of poverty is not the non-attainment of anything external; it comes from having turned away from the self. And so this feeling cannot be eradicated by anything outer; it can only be erased from within.

The nature of the self is bliss. It is not a quality of the self, it is its very essence. Happiness is not a relationship with the self; the self is bliss itself. They are just two names for the same truth. What we call the self is bliss from the experiential point of view, so be careful not to confuse what you know as happiness with real happiness. Real happiness is the self itself. When this has been attained, the search for all else ceases. Achieving a false kind of happiness only intensifies the search, and the fear of losing this so-called happiness disturbs one's peace of mind. Water that increases one's thirst is not really water at all. Christ said, "Come, let me lead you to the well whose water will quench your thirst forever."

We continuously mistake pleasure for happiness. Pleasure is only a shadow, only the reflection of happiness. But most people exist in the illusion that this phantom of happiness is what life is all about. And naturally, they are ultimately disillusioned. It is like mistaking the reflection of the moon for the moon itself and trying to grab hold of it. The deeper you dive into a lake to find the moon, the farther and farther away you go from the real moon.

And in the same way, in their search for pleasure, people move farther and farther away from happiness. This path only leads to misery. Do you see the truth in what I am saying? Surely your own life must bear witness to the fact that the race after pleasure only leads to unhappiness. But this is quite natural. A reflection is outwardly identical to the original, but it is not the real thing at all.

All pleasures hold out the promise of happiness and give one the assurance that they are happiness itself—but pleasure is only the shadow of happiness. Accepting pleasure as happiness can only result in failure and in feelings of remorse. How can I catch you by trying to grab your shadow? And even if I did catch your shadow, what would I have in my hands?

Let me also remind you that a reflection is always opposite to what it is reflecting. If I stand in front of a mirror, my reflected image is exactly opposite to the way I am really standing. This is also true of pleasure. It is just the reflection of happiness. Happiness is an inner quality; pleasure is an outer manifestation, only existing in the material world.

Only happiness is bliss. Continue your pursuit of pleasure, and you will discover for yourselves the truth of what I am saying. All pleasure ends in misery.

But what something becomes at the end, it was at the beginning as well. Because your vision does not penetrate deeply enough, what you should be able to perceive at the beginning is only apparent to you at the end. It is just not possible that what is revealed at the end of some event was not also present at the outset. The end is but a development of the beginnings. What was hidden in the beginning is manifest at the end.

But you see things in reverse order—if indeed you see anything at all. Over and over again, you keep on following paths that lead you to misery, pain, and remorse. Why does man do the same things over and over again when he ends up in misery every time? Why? Perhaps it is because he sees no other path before him. That is why I say your sight is dim and distorted; that is why I question whether you have any sight at all.

There are very few people who actually use their eyes. Everyone has two eyes, but in spite of them, most people are blind. The person who does not see within himself has not yet used his eyes. Only the one who has seen the self can really say he has used his eyes. If a man is not able to see his self, will he ever really be able to see anything?

My friends, your ability to see only begins when you see the self. When a person has seen his self, he begins to move in the direction of happiness. He turns toward pleasure no longer. And others can feel this change in him. The direction of pleasure is from one's self toward the world; the direction of happiness is from the world toward the self.

—Osho

A Note About Language

Spoken Words: Osho's books are not "written," but rather are transcribed from recordings of his talks. These talks are extemporaneous, without reference to notes other than copies of questions, stories, or scriptures he has been asked to comment upon, or jokes he might use to drive home a particular point. He has asked his editors to preserve that quality of the spoken word in his printed books.

Pronouns: When hearing him speak, it is quite clear to the listener that generally when Osho talks about "man," he is referring to "human beings." His use of "he" as a default pronoun simply serves an ease and flow of speaking—in no way does it imply that "she" (or "they") is being dismissed or disregarded.

Osho's unique vantage point is good to keep in mind: *A meditator is neither a man nor a woman, because meditation has nothing to do with your body; neither does it have anything to do with your mind. In meditation you are simply and purely consciousness. And consciousness is neither male nor female.*

The Forgotten Language
of Ecstasy

Ecstasy is a language that man has completely forgotten. He has been forced to forget it; he has been compelled to forget it. The society is against it; the civilization is against it. The society has a tremendous investment in misery. It depends on misery; it feeds on misery; it survives on misery. The society is not for human beings. The society is using human beings as a means for itself. The society has become more important than humanity. The culture, the civilization, the church—they all have become more important. They were meant to be for man, but now they are not for man. They have almost reversed the whole process: now man exists for them.

Every child is born ecstatic. Ecstasy is natural. It is not something that happens only to great sages. It is something that everybody brings with him into the world; everybody comes with it. It is life's innermost core. It is part of being alive. Life is ecstasy. Every child brings it into the world, but then the society jumps on the child, starts destroying the possibility of ecstasy, starts making the child miserable, starts conditioning the child.

The society is neurotic, and it cannot allow ecstatic people to be here. They are dangerous for it. Try to understand the mechanism; then things will be easier.

You cannot control an ecstatic man; it is impossible. You can only control a miserable man. An ecstatic man is bound to be free. Ecstasy is freedom. He cannot be reduced to being a slave. You cannot destroy him so easily; you cannot persuade him to live in a prison. He would like to dance under the stars and he would like to walk with the wind and he would like to talk with the sun and the moon. He will need the vast, the infinite, the huge, the enormous. He cannot be seduced into living in a dark cell. You cannot make a slave out of him. He will live his own life, and he will do his thing. This is very difficult for the society. If there are many ecstatic people, the society will feel it is falling apart, its structure will not hold anymore.

Those ecstatic people will be the rebels. Remember, I don't call an ecstatic person "revolutionary"; I call him a "rebel." A revolutionary is one who wants to change the society, but he wants to replace it with another society. A rebel is one who wants to live as an individual and would like there to exist no rigid social structure in the world. A rebel is one who does not want to replace this society with another society—because all the societies have proved the same. The capitalist and the communist

> Ecstasy is rebellious. It is not revolutionary.

and the fascist and the socialist—they are all cousin-brothers; it doesn't make much difference. The society is society. All the churches have proved the same—the Hindu, the Christian, the Mohammedan.

Once a structure becomes powerful, it does not want anybody to be ecstatic, because ecstasy is against structure. Listen to it and meditate over it: ecstasy is against structure. Ecstasy is rebellious. It is not revolutionary.

A revolutionary is a political man; a rebel is a religious man. A revolutionary wants another structure, of his own desire, of his own utopia, but a structure all the same. He wants to be in power. He wants to be the oppressor and not the oppressed; he wants to be the exploiter and not the exploited. He wants to rule and not be ruled. A rebel is one who neither wants to be ruled nor wants to rule. A rebel is one who wants no rule in the world. A rebel is anarchic. A rebel is one who trusts nature, not man-made structures, who trusts that if nature is left alone, everything will be beautiful. It is!

Such a vast universe goes on without any government. Animals, birds, trees, everything goes on without any government. Why does man need government? Something must have gone wrong. Why is man so neurotic that he cannot live without rulers?

Now there is a vicious circle.

> Man can live without rulers, but he has never been given any opportunity—the rulers won't give you any opportunity.

Man can live without rulers, but he has never been given any opportunity—the rulers won't give you any opportunity. Once you know you can live without the rulers, who would like them to be there? Who will support them? Right now you are supporting your own enemies. You go on voting for your own enemies. Two enemies stand in a presidential contest, and you choose. Both are the same. It is as if you are given freedom to choose the prison, which prison you want to go in. And you vote happily—that I would like to go to prison A or B, that I believe in the Republican prison, I believe in the Democratic prison. But both are prisons. And once you support a prison, the prison has its own investment. Then it will not allow you to have a taste of freedom.

So, from the very childhood, the child is not allowed to taste freedom, because once he knows what freedom is, then he will not concede, he will not compromise—then he will not be ready to live in any dark cell. He would like to die, but he will not allow anybody to reduce him to being a slave. He will be assertive. Of course he will not be interested in becoming powerful over other people. These are neurotic trends, when you are too interested in becoming powerful over people. That simply shows that deep down you are powerless, and you are afraid that if you don't become powerful, others are going to overpower you.

Machiavelli says that the best way of defense is to attack. The best way to protect yourself is to attack first. These so-called politicians all over the world—in the East, in the West—are all deep down very weak people, suffering from inferiority, afraid that if they don't become powerful politically, then somebody is going to exploit them, so why not exploit rather than be exploited? The exploited and the exploiter, both are sailing in the same boat—and both are helping the boat, protecting the boat.

> Once the child knows the taste of freedom, he will never become part of any society, any church, any club, any political party.

Once the child knows the taste of freedom, he will never become part of any society, any church, any club, any political party. He will remain an individual, he will remain free, and he will create pulsations of freedom around him. His very being will become a door to freedom.

The child is not allowed to taste freedom. If the child asks the mother, "Mom, can I go outside? The sun is beautiful and the air is very crisp and I would like to run around the block," immediately— obsessively, compulsively—the mother says, "No!" The child has not asked much. He just wanted to go out into the morning sun, into the brisk air, he wanted to enjoy the sunlight and the air and the company of the trees—he has not asked for anything!—but compulsively, out of some deep compulsion, the mother says no. It is very difficult to hear a mother saying yes, very difficult to hear a father saying yes. Even if they say yes, they say so very reluctantly. Even if they say yes, they make the child feel that he is guilty, that he is forcing them, that he is doing something wrong.

Whenever the child feels happy, doing whatsoever, somebody or other is bound to come and stop him—"Don't do this!" By and by the child understands, "Whatsoever I feel happy in is wrong." And, of course, he never feels happy doing what others tell him to do, because it is not a spontaneous urge in him. So he comes to know that to be miserable is right, to be happy is wrong. That becomes the deep association.

If he wants to open the clock and see inside, the whole family jumps on him—"Stop! You will destroy the clock. This is not good." He was just looking into the clock; it was a scientific curiosity. He wanted to see what makes it tick. It was perfectly okay. And the clock is not so valuable as his curiosity, as his inquiring mind. The clock is worthless—even if it is destroyed, nothing is destroyed—but once the inquiring mind is destroyed, much is destroyed; then he will never inquire for truth.

Or it is a beautiful night and the sky is full of stars and the child wants to sit outside, but it is time to go to sleep. He is not feeling sleepy at all; he is wide-awake, very, very much awake. The child is puzzled. In the morning, when he feels sleepy, everybody is after him—"Get up!" When he was enjoying, when it was so beautiful to be in the bed, when he wanted to take another turn and have a little more sleep and dream a little more, then everybody was against him: "Get up! It is time to get up." Now he is wide-awake, and he wants to enjoy the stars. It is very poetic, this moment, very romantic. He feels thrilled. How can he go to sleep in such a thrill? He is so excited, he wants to sing and dance, and they are forcing him to go to sleep—"It is nine o'clock. It is time to go to sleep."

Now, he was happy being awake, but he is forced to go to sleep. When he is playing, he is forced to come to the dining table. He is not hungry. When he is hungry, the mother says, "This is not the time." This way we go on destroying all possibility of being ecstatic, all possibility of being happy, joyful, delighted. Whatsoever the child feels spontaneously happy with seems to be wrong, and whatsoever he does not feel at all seems to be right.

In the school, a bird suddenly starts singing outside the classroom, and the child is all attention toward the bird, of course—not toward the mathematics teacher, who is standing at the board with his ugly chalk. But the teacher is more powerful, politically more powerful, than the bird. Certainly, the bird has no power, but it has beauty. The bird attracts the child without hammering on his head, "Be attentive! Concentrate toward me!" No—simply, spontaneously, naturally, the consciousness of the child starts flowing out of the window. It goes to the bird. His heart is there, but he has to look at the blackboard. There is nothing to look at, but he has to pretend.

Happiness is wrong. Wherever there is happiness, the child starts becoming afraid something is going to be wrong. If the child is playing with his own body, it is wrong. If the child is playing with his own sexual organs, it is wrong. And that is one of the most ecstatic moments in the life of a child. He enjoys his body; it is thrilling. But all thrill has to be cut, all joy has to be destroyed. It is neurotic, but the society is neurotic.

The same was done to the parents by their parents; the same they are doing to their children. This way one generation goes on destroying another. This way we transfer our neurosis from one generation to another. The whole earth has become a madhouse. Nobody seems to know what ecstasy is. It is lost. Barriers upon barriers have been created.

It is a daily observation here that when people start meditating and they start feeling the upsurge of energy and when they start feeling happy, they immediately come to me and say, "A very strange thing is happening. I am feeling happy, and I am also feeling guilty, for no reason at all." Guilty? They are also puzzled. Why should one feel guilty? They know that there is nothing— they have not done anything wrong. From where does this guilt arise? It is coming from that deep-rooted conditioning that joy is wrong. To be sad is okay, but to be happy is not allowed.

Once I used to live in a town. The police commissioner was my friend; we were friends from the university student days. He used to come to me, and he would say, "I am so miserable. Help me to come out of it." I would say, "You talk about coming out of it, but I don't see that you really want to come out of it. In the first place, why have you chosen to work in this police department? You must be miserable, and you want others also to be miserable."

One day I asked three of my disciples to go around the town and dance in different parts of the town and be happy. They said, "For what?" I said, "You simply go." Within one hour, of course, they were caught by the police. I called the police commissioner; I said, "Why have you caught these people of mine?"

He said, "These people seem to be mad."

I asked him, "Have they done anything wrong? Have they harmed anybody?"

He said, "No, nothing. Really, they have not done anything wrong."

"Then why have you caught them?"

He said, "But they were dancing on the streets! And they were laughing."

"But if they have not done anything harmful to anybody, why should you interfere? Why should you come in? They have not attacked anybody; they have not entered anybody's territory. They were just dancing. Innocent people, laughing."

He said, "You are right, but it is dangerous."

"Why is it dangerous? To be happy is dangerous? To be ecstatic is dangerous?"

He got the point; he immediately released them. He came running to me; he said, "You may be right. I cannot allow myself to be happy, and I cannot allow anybody else to be happy."

These are your politicians; these are your police commissioners; these are your magistrates. The juries, your leaders, your so-called saints, your priests, your popes—these are the people. They all have a great investment in your misery. They depend on your misery. If you are miserable, they are happy.

Only a miserable person will go to the temple to pray. A happy person will go to a temple? For what? A happy person is so happy that he feels God everywhere! That's what happiness is all about. He's so ecstatically in love with existence that wherever he looks he finds

> Only a miserable person will go to the temple to pray.

9

God. Everywhere is his temple. And wherever he bows down, suddenly he finds God's feet, nothing else. His awe, his reverence, need not be so narrow that he has to go to a Hindu temple or a Christian church. That is silly; that is meaningless. Only miserable people who cannot see God, who cannot see God in a blooming flower, who cannot see God in a singing bird, who cannot see God in a psychedelic rainbow, who cannot see God in the floating clouds, who cannot see God in the rivers and in the ocean, who cannot see God in the beautiful eyes of a child, they go to the church, they go to the mosque, they go to the temple, they go to the priest, and they ask, "Where is God? Please show us."

Only miserable people become available to religions. Yes, Bertrand Russell was almost right when he said that if someday the world becomes happy, religion will disappear. I say *almost* right, ninety-nine percent right. I cannot say a hundred percent right because I know of another type of religion which Bertrand Russell is not aware of. Yes, these religions will disappear—he is right about these religions: the Hindu, the Christian, the Mohammedan, the Jain, the Buddhist, these will disappear—certainly they will disappear. If the world becomes happy, they are bound to disappear, because who will bother? But he is only ninety-nine percent right; he is one percent wrong. And that one percent is more important than the ninety-nine percent because another type of religion, *real* religion—ecstatic religion, religion which has no name, religion which has no code, no Bible, no Koran, no Vedas, a religion which has no scripture, no adjective to it, just a religion of dance, a religion of love, a religion of reverence, a religion of benediction, *pure* religion—will arise in the world when people are happy.

In fact, these religions that exist, they are not religions. They are just sedatives, tranquilizers. Marx is also right of course—only ninety-nine percent—that religion is the opium of the masses. He is right. These religions help you to tolerate your misery. They help you, they console you, they give you hope that "Yes, today you are miserable; tomorrow you will be happy." And that to-morrow never comes. They say, "In this life, you are miserable, but in the next life . . . Be good, be moral, follow the rules of the society—be a slave, be obedient—and in the next life you will be happy." And nobody knows about the next life. Nobody ever comes and says anything about it. Or if they don't believe in the next life, they say, "When you have gone to the other shore, to heaven, there is your reward." But be obedient to the priest and the politician.

> There is a conspiracy
> between the priest
> and the politician.

There is a conspiracy between the priest and the politician. They are two sides of the same coin. They help each other. And they all are interested in you remaining miserable—so the priest can have a congregation and the priest can exploit you, and the politician can force you to go to wars in the name of the nation, in the name of the state, in the name of this and that—and it is all nonsense, but he can send you to war. Only miserable people can be enlisted for war; only deeply miserable people can be ready to fight, can be ready to kill and to be killed. They are so miserable that even death seems to be better than their life.

I have heard Adolf Hitler was talking to a British diplomat. They were standing on the thirtieth floor of a skyscraper, and to impress him, he ordered one German soldier to jump off. And the soldier simply jumped without even hesitating, and, of course, died. The British diplomat could not believe it; it was unbelievable. He was very much shocked. This wastage? For no reason at all. And to impress him more, Hitler ordered another soldier, "Jump!" and the other jumped. And to impress him even more, he ordered a third soldier.

By this time, the diplomat had come to his senses. He rushed and stopped the soldier and said, "What are you doing, destroying your life for no reason at all?" He said, "Who wants to live, sir, in this country and under this madman? Who wants to live with this Adolf Hitler? It is better to die! It is freedom."

When people are miserable, death seems to be freedom. And when people are miserable, they are so full of rage, anger, that they want to kill—even if the risk is that they may be killed. The politician exists because you are miserable. So Vietnam can continue, Bangladesh, the Arab countries. War continues. Somewhere or other, war continues.

This state of affairs has to be understood—why it exists and how you can drop out of it. Unless you drop out of it, unless you understand the whole mechanism, the conditioning—the hypnosis in which you are living—unless you take hold of it, watch it, and drop it, you will never become ecstatic, and you will never be able to sing the song that you have come to sing.

Then you will die without singing your song. Then you will die without dancing your dance. Then you will die without having ever lived.

Your life is just a hope; it is not a reality. It can be a reality.

The Poison of Ambition

This neurosis that you call society, civilization, culture, education, this neurosis has a subtle structure. The structure is this: it gives you symbolic ideas so that reality by and by is clouded, becomes clouded, you can't see the real, and you start becoming attached to the unreal. For example, the society tells you to be ambitious; it helps you to become ambitious. Ambition means living in hope, living in the tomorrow. Ambition means today has to be sacrificed for tomorrow.

Today is all that is there; now is the only time you are, you ever will be. If you want to live, it is now or never.

> Happiness is not an achievement. It is your nature.

Society makes you ambitious. From the very childhood when you go to school and ambition is put into you, you are poisoned: grow rich, become powerful, become somebody. Nobody tells you that you already have the capacity to be happy. Everybody says that you can have the capacity to be happy only if you fulfill certain conditions—that you have enough money, a big house, a big car, and this and that—only then can you be happy.

Happiness has nothing to do with these things. Happiness is not an achievement. It is your nature. Animals are happy without any money. They are not Rockefellers. And no Rockefeller is as happy as a deer or a dog. Animals have no political power—they are not prime ministers and presidents—but they are happy. The trees are happy; otherwise they would have stopped blooming. They still bloom; the spring still comes. They still dance, they still sing, they still pour their being into the feet of the divine. Their prayer is continuous; their worship is always happening. And they don't go to any church; there is no need. God comes to them. In the wind, in the rain, in the sun, God comes to them.

Only man is not happy, because man lives in ambition and not in reality. Ambition is a trick. It is a trick to distract your mind. Symbolic life has been substituted for real life.

Watch it in life. The mother cannot love the child as much as the child wants the mother to love him, because the mother is hung up in her head. Her life has not been one of fulfillment. Her love life has been a disaster. She has not been able to flower. She has lived in ambition. She has tried to control her man, possess him. She has been jealous. She has not been a loving woman. If she has not been a loving woman, how can she suddenly be loving to the child?

I was just reading a book of R.D. Laing. He sent me his new book just two, three days ago, *The Facts of Life*. In the book he refers to an experiment in which a psychoanalyst asked many mothers, "When your child was going to be born, were you really in a welcome mood, were you ready to accept the child?" He had made a questionnaire. First question: "Was the child accidental or did you desire the child?" Ninety percent of the women said, "It was accidental; we did not desire it." Then, "When the pregnancy happened, were you hesitant? Did you want the child, or did you want an abortion? Were you clear about it?" Many of them said that they hesitated for months whether to have an abortion or have the child. Then the child was born—they could not decide. Maybe other considerations—maybe the religious consideration: it may create sin for them; it may create hell for them. They may have been Catholics or Hindus or Jainas, and the idea of violence, that abortion is violence, prevented them from getting an abortion. Or social considerations. Or the husband wanted it. Or they would like to have a child as a continuity of their ego. But the child was not liked. Rarely was there a mother who said, "Yes, the child was welcome. I was waiting for him, and I was happy." And even of those who said this, the psychiatrist writes, "We were not certain whether they were being honest. They may have been just saying so."

Now a child is born who is unwelcome. From the very beginning, the mother has been hesitating whether to have it or not to have it. There must be repercussions. The child must feel these tensions. When the mother would think to abort the child, the child must have felt hurt. The child is part of the mother's body; every vibe will reach the child. Or when the mother thinks and hesitates and is just in a limbo of what to do or what not to do, the child will also feel a trembling, shaking—he is hanging between death and life. And then somehow the child is born, and the mother thinks it is just accidental—they had tried birth control, they had tried this and that, and everything failed and the child is there—so one has to tolerate. That tolerance is not love.

The child misses love from the very beginning. And the mother also feels guilty because she is not giving as much love as there would have been naturally. So she starts substituting. She forces the child to eat too much. She cannot fill the child's soul with love; she tries to stuff his body with food. It is a substitute. You can go and see. Mothers are so obsessive. The child says, "I am not hungry," and the mothers go on forcing. They have nothing to do with the child; they don't listen to the child. They are substituting: they cannot give love, so they give food. Then the child grows: they cannot love; they give money. Money becomes a substitute for love.

And the child also learns that money is more important than love. If you don't have love, nothing to be worried about, but you must have money. In life he will become greedy. He will go after money like a maniac. He will not bother about love. He will say, "First things first. I should first have a big balance in the bank. I must have this much money; only then can I afford love."

Now, love needs no money; you can love as you are. And if you think love needs money, and you go after money, one day you may have money, and then suddenly you will feel empty because all the years were wasted in accumulating money. And they are not only wasted! All those years were years of no love, so you have practiced no love. Now the money is there, but you don't know how to love. You have forgotten the very language of feeling, the language of love, the language of ecstasy.

Yes, you can purchase a beautiful woman, but that is not love. You can purchase the most beautiful woman of the world, but that is not love. And she will be coming to you not because she loves you; she will be coming to you because of your bank balance.

Mulla Nasruddin was in love with a woman—very homely and ordinary, but she had much money and she was the only child of her father, and the father was old and dying. Mulla was deeply in love with the woman, and one day he went to her very excitedly because the father was approaching death very fast, and he said, "I am dying."

Mulla said to the woman, "I am dying; I cannot live without you a single moment."

She said, "That's okay, but I have bad news for you. My father has made a will, and he has given all his money to a trust and I am not going to get any money. Mulla, do you love me still?"

Mulla said, "I love you, and I will always love you though I will never see you again. But I will always love you, and I will always remember you!"

All love disappears. This is symbolic; money is a symbol. Power, political power, is a symbol. Respectability is a symbol. These are not realities; these are human projections. These are not objectives; they have no objectivity. They are not there. They are just dreams projected by a miserable mind. If you want to be ecstatic, you will have to drop out of the symbolic. To be freed of the symbolic is to be freed of the society. To be freed of the symbolic is to become a seeker of truth. To be freed of the symbolic, you have taken courage to enter into the real. And only the real is real. The symbolic is not real.

More of the Heart, Less of the Head

What is ecstasy? Something to be achieved? No. Something that you have to earn? No. Something that you have to become? No. Ecstasy is being, and becoming is misery. If you want to become something, you will be miserable. Becoming is the very root cause of misery. If you want to be ecstatic—then it is just now, herenow, this very moment. Look at me. This very moment—nobody is barring the path—you can be happy. Happiness is so obvious and so easy. It's your nature. You are already carrying it. Just give it a chance to flower, to bloom.

> Ecstasy is being, and becoming is misery.

Ecstasy is not of the head, remember. Ecstasy is of the heart. Ecstasy is not of thought; it is of feeling. And you have been deprived of feeling. You have been cut away from feeling. You don't know what feeling is. Even when you say, "I feel," you only think you feel. When you say, "I am feeling happy," watch, analyze, and you will find you *think* you are feeling happy. Even feeling has to pass through thinking. It has to pass through the censor of thinking; only when thinking approves of it is it allowed. If thinking does not approve of it, it is thrown into the unconscious, into the basement of your being, and forgotten.

Become more of the heart, less of the head. Head is just a part; heart is your whole being. Heart is your totality. So whenever you are total in anything, you function from feeling. Whenever you are partial in anything, you function from the head.

Watch a painter painting—and that is the difference between a real artist and a technician. If the painter is just a technician who knows the technique of how to paint, who knows the know-how, who knows all about colors and the brushes and the canvas, and who has gone through the training, he will function through the head. He will be a technician. He will paint, but he will not be totally in it. Then watch a real artist who is not a technician. He will be absorbed in it, drunk. He will not only paint with his hand, and he will not only paint from his head. He will paint with his whole being: his guts will be involved in it, his feet as much, his blood and bones as much, his marrow. Everything will be involved in it. You can watch it, you can see, you can feel he is totally in it, lost. Nothing else exists. He is drunk. In that moment, he is no more. He is not a doer. The head is a doer. In that moment of total absorption, he is not a doer; he is just a passage, as if God is painting through him.

When you come across a dancer—a *real* dancer, not one who is a performer—then you will see that she is not dancing, no. Something of the beyond is dancing in her. She is totally in it.

It is said about the great dancer Nijinsky that there were moments when he would take such a leap that it was physically impossible—gravitation does not allow that big a leap. He was asked again and again, "How do you do it?" and he would say, "I am surprised as much as you are surprised. And I cannot *manage* to do it. When I try to do it, it never happens, I fall very short, but when I am in the dance and I am completely lost—when I am not!—it happens, as if gravitation suddenly is no more. I become weightless, I don't feel any weight—as if something starts pulling me upwards rather than downwards."

This pull upwards is known in yoga as levitation. Yes, it happens in meditation too. Nijinsky was unknowingly moving into deep meditation. The dance was so total that he became a meditator and levitation happened.

Whenever you are totally into something, you are ecstatic. When you are partially into something, you will remain miserable, because a part will be moving separately from the whole. There will be a division—a split, a tension, anxiety.

> Whenever you are totally into something, you are ecstatic.

If you love from the head, your love is not going to give any ecstatic experience. If you meditate from your head . . .

Just the other night, one woman from the West was saying to me that she has come here because she has seen many people coming here, whose lives have been transformed and who have become so happy. That's why she has also come here—to become happy. She is meditating, but nothing is happening. She is trying hard, but nothing is happening. I told her, "Nothing is going to happen. You start from a very wrong place. Your motivation is the barrier: you have come from the head. Those people had not come with a motive, with greed. You have come with a motive, with greed. Your mind is already poisoned; you have come with an idea, and you are watching for when it is going to happen. It will never happen, because you will never allow yourself to be totally in it. A watcher will stand by the side and will see, has it happened yet or not?"

> Swimming can become a meditation, running can become a meditation— anything can become a meditation.

I used to go to a river to swim, and I loved it. Whenever I would come back, one of my neighbors always used to watch me, and he would see that I was very ecstatic. One day he asked, "What is happening? I always see you going to the river, and for hours you swim in the river and you remain in the river. I am also coming because you look so happy." I said, "Please don't come. You will miss, and the river will be very sad. No, don't come, because your very motivation will be a barrier. You can swim, but you will be watching for when that happiness is going to happen. It will never happen— because it happens only when you are not."

Swimming can become a meditation, running can become a meditation—anything can become a meditation—if you are not. Ecstasy is of the heart, is of the total.

Separation Makes You Miserable

Now look at this: misery separates you; separation makes you miserable. They are together; they are one package. Whenever you are miserable, you suddenly become separate. That's why the ego cannot afford to be happy, because if you become happy, the ego cannot exist—you are no longer separate. The egoist cannot afford to be ecstatic. How can he afford to be ecstatic, because in ecstasy, the ego will not be there? That is too much. He would like to remain miserable. He will create a thousand and one miseries around him just to help the ego to be there.

> When you are miserable, you want to be alone; when you are happy, you want to share.

Have you watched it? When you are really happy, your ego disappears. When you are really happy, suddenly you feel a deep at-one-ment with the whole. When you are miserable, you want to be alone; when you are happy, you want to share.

When Buddha was miserable, he went to the forest, escaped from the world. What happened after six years? When he became ecstatic, he came back, back to the marketplace. When Mahavir was unhappy, miserable, he escaped from the world, he renounced the world. When he became happy, he came back to the world.

Now, Jainas don't talk about Mahavir coming back to the world; they only talk about the renunciation. Their scriptures only say that he renounced the world. That is only half the story—and not the peak, just the beginning of the story. Yes, for twelve years he lived alone in the forest, not uttering a single word. He was so miserable, he separated himself from the whole world. He remained lonely. Then one day came the spring and the flowers started blooming and he was full of ecstasy; he came back to the world. The Jaina scriptures don't talk about it—and that is the real part of the story, the more significant part that he comes back to the world, that he moves amid people, that then again he starts talking, then again he starts singing, then again he conveys, shares. Whatsoever he has attained has to be shared.

In misery you are like a seed. In ecstasy you become a flower, and your fragrance, of course, has to be released to the winds.

You can watch it in your life also, in a small way, of course. When you are unhappy, you close your doors, you don't want to see your friends, you don't want to go anywhere, you don't want to participate in anything. You say, "Leave me alone. Please leave me alone." When somebody becomes very, very unhappy, he commits suicide. What is the meaning of it? What is suicide? Suicide is just an effort to go so far away from the world that one cannot come back. It is moving into loneliness *absolutely*, irrevocably, so that you cannot come back. That's what suicide is.

Have you ever heard about any man committing suicide when he was happy, when he was ecstatic, when he was dancing? No, when the dance arises, you burst forth, you throw your doors open, you call your friends, you call your neighbors, and you say, "Come. I am going to give a feast, and let us dance and let us have a little fun. I have much to share, and I would like to give it to you." And whosoever comes to your door, you greet him, you welcome him. Anybody is welcome in the moment when you are happy. When you are unhappy, even those who have always been welcome are no longer welcome.

Let Creativity Be Your Prayer

"God is the creator"—all the religions of the world have been talking about it, but nobody seems to have understood rightly what it means, what is its implication. "God is the creator"—if it is true, then only through creation can you arrive close to him; there is no other way. If God is the creator, then become creative, and creativeness will be your prayer. Paint, sing, dance, compose poetry, make a statue—anything—but become creative. Plant a garden. Anything—small, big, whatsoever. The proportion is not the question—anything, but be creative.

If you are cooking in the kitchen, then cook creatively, then make it more and more artful. Then don't just go on doing it in a routine way. Let it be your poetry, your sculpture, let it be your song. Whatsoever you are doing, be creative, bring the new in. Go on exploring the unknown. Innovate, invent, discover, create something—because if God is the creator, then whenever you become creative, you come close to him. Whenever you are creative, God is the creator in you.

But up to now the religious people have lived very uncreatively; they don't create. They simply remove themselves from the world. They don't compose poems; they don't paint pictures; they don't carve statues. They simply become aloof; they become uncreative. To become uncreative is to go against God.

A story:

I have heard about a soldier in the Second World War who would drop his rifle on the battlefield and run to pick up any little scrap of paper, would examine it eagerly, then sorrowfully shake his head as the paper fluttered to the ground. Hospitalized, he remained mute, his compulsion obscure and intractable. He wandered forlornly about the psychiatric ward, picking up scraps of paper, each time with discernable hope followed by inevitable dejection. Pronounced unfit for service, he received one day his discharge from the army, whereupon, receiving the discharge form, he found his voice. "This is it!" he cried in ecstasy. "This is it!"

Ecstasy is the ultimate freedom, and then one simply shouts in joy, "This is it! This is it! Eureka! I have found it."

And the irony is that you need not go anywhere to find it. It is already there. It is your very core, your very being. If you decide to find it, you can find it this very moment. It does not need a single moment's postponement. An intense thirst can open the door. A great urgency can right now make you free.

The Closest Mystery
Is Your Own

A Sufi story:

The philosophers, logicians, and doctors of law were drawn up at court to examine Mulla Nasruddin. This was a serious case because he had admitted going from village to village saying, "The so-called wise men are ignorant, irresolute, and confused." He was charged with undermining the security of the state.

"You may speak first," said the king.

"Have paper and pens brought," said the Mulla. Paper and pens were brought. "Give some to each of the first seven savants." They were distributed. "Have them write separately an answer to this question: What is bread?" This was done. The papers were handed to the king, who read them out.

The first said, "Bread is a food."

The second, "It is flour and water."

The third, "A gift of God."

The fourth, "Baked dough."

The fifth, "Changeable, according to how you mean *bread*."

The sixth, "A nutritious substance."

The seventh, "Nobody really knows."

"When they decide what bread is," said Nasruddin, "it will be possible for them to decide other things. For example, whether I am right or wrong. Can you entrust matters of assessment and judgment to people like this? Is it or is it not strange that they cannot agree about something which they eat each day and yet are unanimous that I am a heretic?"

Yes, that is the situation of your so-called philosophers, theologians, doctors of law—the learned people. They are parrots. They have not even known themselves yet. What else can they know? They are not even acquainted with themselves. How can they be acquainted with others? They have not unraveled the mystery that they are.

> Your knowledge becomes a defense: it is a security for your ignorance.

The closest mystery is your own. If even that is not known, how will you know the mystery of the others? Those mysteries are farther away from you; they are distant. The easiest to approach, the most easily approachable, is your own mystery. The journey has to begin from there.

The learned people—the pundits, the scholars, the professors— are only better informed. But information makes no one wise. Yes, it helps you to pretend wisdom. It becomes a camouflage; it is a facade behind which you can hide your ignorance. But the ignorance is not destroyed by it; on the contrary, it is protected.

Your knowledge becomes a defense: it is a security for your ignorance; it is nourishment. You become fully unaware that you are ignorant; that is the purpose of your so-called knowledge.

> When you use words like *God*, do you know what you are saying?

And this is dangerous. If you are unaware that you are ill, then there is no possibility of searching for health. If you become oblivious of the fact of your fundamental ignorance, how are you ever going to become enlightened? If you have forgotten that your interior is full of darkness, you will not search for light; you will not work to create light. If you have already accepted that you know, then what is the point of going on an adventure of knowing?

And that's what your so-called knowledge goes on doing. It does not change the ignorant person into a knowing person; it only gives an illusion of knowledge. It is a mirage. It is a dream in which you become wise. But in reality, you remain the same.

The difference between the ignorant and the so-called learned is only of quantity. No qualitative difference at all exists between them. The ignorant is less informed, less polished, less educated. The learned is more informed, more educated, has read more, has listened to more people. The difference is of language. The learned is more articulate, knows many more words. But they are mere words, remember. There is no meaning in them; there cannot be any meaning in them, because meaning comes through experience.

You can learn all the great words—they are in the dictionaries. That's how you go on using words. When you use words like *God*, do you know what you are saying? Do you know what you mean? What is God? It is a mere word for you, and it will remain a mere word. But behind the word there is a danger; you may start believing that you know because you know the word.

Knowing the word *God* is not knowing God. Knowing the word *love* is not knowing love. Knowing the word *fire* is not knowing fire. Remember, words are mere symbols. Unless you pour existential meaning into them, they will remain empty. There is no meaning in the words; the meaning is in the individual and his experience.

If Krishna uses the word *God*, it is not a mere word. It is meaningful, it has significance. The significance comes from Krishna's life; the significance is poured from Krishna's consciousness. When Jesus uses the word *God*, it is of utter import, it is pregnant with great meaning. The meaning is in Jesus, not in the word *God*, because the word *God* has been used by rabbis, down the ages, with no meaning at all. Jesus poured meaning into it. He transformed an empty word into a significant, meaningful, alive thing; it started pulsating. When Buddha touched any word, it became alive, it grew wings. Suddenly there was a metamorphosis.

But the learned is only full of dust, the dust that he has gathered from books, scriptures. Beware of such learning; it is more dangerous than simple ignorance. Why is it more dangerous than ignorance? Because ignorance has a purity. It has innocence in it, and it has an authenticity. It is true, and from truth there is a possibility to go further. Knowledge, the so-called knowledge, is untrue. From untruth you cannot go on a journey of truth.

Remember, there is no actual difference between the learned and the ignorant, except that the learned believes that he knows, and the ignorant knows that he does not know. But then the ignorant is in a better position.

An American lady who speaks no French takes her little daughter to the Paris zoo. They stop in front of a cage with porcupines inside and read a sign that says, Porcupi Africain, Porcupi Australian.

This puzzles them, because the porcupines all look just about the same. So the mother goes up to the guard, who is standing nearby, and says, "Monsieur, do you speak English?"

The guard touches his cap and says, "Madame, I speak only very little English. What is it Madame wishes to know?"

"Would you tell us please what is the difference between the Australian porcupine and the African porcupine?"

"It is this, Madame: the prick of the African porcupine is longer than the prick of the Australian porcupine."

The lady is horrified and rushes off with her daughter until she finds the superintendent of the zoo.

"Monsieur," she says, "do you speak English?"

"Madame," says the superintendent, "I have been speaking English for many years. I have studied at Oxford, and,

*in fact, I can speak as well as you. What does Madame wish
to know?"*

*So she tells him with great indignation the awful thing
that the guard has just said in front of her and her little girl.*

*"Madame must not be offended," says the superintendent.
"You see, what the guard is trying to say is that the quill of
the African porcupine is longer that the quill of the Australian
porcupine. For as a matter of fact, Madame, their pricks are
the same size."*

There is not much difference between the so-called learned
and the unlearned. Maybe the difference is of words, of language,
but not of any quality. Their inner quality remains the same.

This is one of the fundamentals to be understood—knowledge
is futile if it has not arisen in your own experience. Knowledge is
an utterly unnecessary burden if it is not part of your own life. If
it is added to you from the outside, drop it. Don't unnecessarily
carry it. It is useless, it is harmful, it is poisonous and a burden.
It will not allow you to move quickly and fast. And the more you
gather knowledge, the less is the possibility of your movement.

Hence your learned people live like stagnant pools; they are
no longer rivers. The learned people go on talking about beautiful words, spinning, weaving great philosophies around them.
But if you go into their words and penetrate deeply, you will
always find emptiness and nothing else.

Great books are written about God by people who have no ink-
ling. Great books are written about heaven and hell; even maps

of heaven and hell have been drawn by people, and they don't know a thing. They have not even penetrated their own world of emotions, feelings; they have not contacted their own inner consciousness. And they are talking about distant things—afterlife, life after death. They are clever people: they know how to talk; they know how to prove; they know how to argue. And they argue in such a beautiful way that anybody can be deceived. If you go into their argument, you will find it very valid. But the validity of the argument is irrelevant. The question is whether the person knows or not.

Sometimes it happens that a person knows but cannot argue or argues faultily. A person sometimes knows but has no language to express it or uses wrong language, but still what he says is true. His argument may be false, his language may not be adequate, but still what he says is true. And on the other extreme there are people whose language you cannot find fault with: their argument is perfect; they are accomplished logicians. You cannot argue with them; they will immediately silence you. Still, what they are saying is utterly stupid, it does not make any sense. It is just in their minds; their hearts are utterly untouched by it. They themselves are not moved by what they are saying! When they talk about God, there is no juice flowing in their being. When they talk about love, you will not see any sign in their eyes, and when they talk about poetry, there is no poetry in their presence. They talk about grace, but you will not see any grace anywhere.

But they can create a great turmoil of words; they can create a great smoke of words. And if you also live in words, there is every possibility you will be deceived. That's how millions of people are lost—the blind are leading those otherwise blind. The articulate blind are leading the inarticulate blind; the informed blind are leading the uninformed blind.

And whenever a man of eyes is born—a Jesus, a Buddha, a Bahauddin, a Hakim Sanai—all those scholars and learned people are immediately in agreement about one thing: that Jesus is wrong. They may not agree about what bread is, they may not agree about anything else, but about one thing they immediately agree: that Jesus is wrong. They may be Hindus; they may be Mohammedans; they may be Jews; they may be somebody else. But when there is a man like Jesus, they immediately all fall into agreement because they all see the risk; if Jesus is right, then they are all wrong. Jesus has to be proved wrong. And if they cannot prove him wrong—and they cannot—then Jesus has to be destroyed. If they cannot prove him wrong, then the only way is to remove Jesus from people's lives.

And once Jesus is killed, the same people who killed Jesus will become Jesus's followers—popes, bishops, and priests. Again they are there to philosophize. With Jesus there is trouble, but with Jesus's words there is no problem. They can spin and weave around any word; whether it is from Moses or Jesus makes no difference to them. Now Jesus becomes their center of philosophizing.

Buddha became the greatest source of philosophers. A strange phenomenon, unbelievable—because Buddha was utterly against philosophy. He remained absolutely anti-philosophy his whole life. He never talked about any philosophical subject. He was down-to-earth; he was a pragmatist, a practical man. If you had asked him about God, he would have immediately pushed the question aside and would have told you, "How is it going to transform you? Talking about God is meaningless; don't waste time. Think about meditation, think about compassion, think about things which can transform you. What can God do?"

If you had asked him about the afterlife, he would have immediately stopped you: "Don't talk nonsense. You are alive and you don't know what life is and you are thinking about the afterlife? You don't know what you are right now and you are asking, 'What will I be after death?' This is utter stupidity. Rather, go into yourself and see who you are. And if you have known yourself, then there is no problem. When you die, you will know whether you survive or not. Why make much fuss about it right now?"

And how can it be decided? There is no way of deciding. Even if the whole world says that you will survive the bodily death, still the doubt will persist. Who knows? Everybody will be wrong— because the whole world used to believe that the earth was flat, and the whole world was wrong. The earth is not flat; now we know. The whole world has believed, down the ages, that the sun moves around the earth. Now we know the earth moves around the sun, not vice versa.

So it is not a question of how many people believe in it. Truth is not decided by the majority, it is not a question of voting. Even if a single man knows truth, and the whole world is against him, he is still true, and the world is still wrong.

You cannot be convinced that you will exist when you are

dead; there is no way of convincing you. You can believe it if you *want* to believe; if you want to believe, you can believe anything. But it is because you want to, not that you are convinced. You are afraid of death; you would like to remain after death, and you want to believe it, so you believe it. But you know that it is your belief; it may not be so. Deep down, the doubt will persist.

And Buddha wouldn't have answered any question that you can think belongs to philosophy. He used to say, "Even if I say something about the beyond, you will misunderstand it. You don't have any experience of the beyond; communication is not possible." And you can see how difficult it is to communicate. I say one thing; you will understand another. People will understand according to their level of understanding.

A playboy who had squandered a fortune was asked what he had done with all his money. He answered, "Some went for liquor and fast automobiles, and most went for women. The rest I spent foolishly."

Words don't mean the same thing to everybody. It is according to your understanding.

"Your continual unfaithfulness proves you are absolutely worthless!" yelled the outraged man who had just caught his wife for the tenth time with another man.

"Quite the contrary," came the cool reply. "It merely proves I am too good to be true."

It all depends on you.

On a foreign business trip, after working hours, a man found himself hampered by the fact that he didn't know the language. He was delighted, therefore, when a gorgeous woman sat down at his restaurant table.

"Can you speak English?" he ventured hopefully.

"Just a little," she said with a smile.

"Just a little, eh?" he repeated. "How much?"

"Twenty-five dollars," was the prompt reply.

Communication is one of the most difficult problems in the world. When you use a word, you give your meaning to it. When it reaches the other person, it is bound to take that other person's meaning. And in the transfer, everything is lost. So Buddha said, "I will not talk about the beyond. And don't ask anything about the beyond. Be more scientific and realistic; go into that which is. Don't talk about 'truth.' Go into that which is, go into that which you are, and that is the way to know truth."

But once Buddha died, great philosophical schools arose. It had never happened in the whole world as it happened in India after Buddha. The man, who for his whole life was against philosophy and philosophizing, became the source of the greatest philosophical endeavor ever. Thirty-six schools of philosophy were born when Buddha died, and the people that had always condemned him all gathered together to philosophize about him. And see the beauty, the irony. They started philosophizing why Buddha kept silent. Why didn't he say anything about the beyond? That became their philosophy! They started talking about why he kept silent about the beyond. And there were as many answers as possible.

Somebody said, "Because there is no beyond." Now one philosophy has taken roots.

Another said, "The beyond is, but it is inexpressible. That's why he kept silent."

Now another school, and so on and so forth.

Even the silence of Buddha became a problem, and people started discussing the silence. Nobody tried to become silent; people started talking about the silence.

Beware of this trap; the mind is very cunning. If I say something about meditation, I am saying it so that you can meditate. But you start thinking about meditation, what meditation is. How many kinds of meditation are there? What is the difference between them? Why are they antagonistic to each other? And then you can go on ad infinitum, and there will not be any time when you will ever meditate. You will become more and more confused. You will become so confused, finally, that you will not know how to start meditation, because there are so many directions opening. Where to go? What to choose? You will simply be paralyzed.

The mind always does that. And only a few people who are really alert are capable to get out of these traps of the mind. The mind is a great philosopher. And life is not a philosophy; life is a reality. Philosophy is an escape from reality; philosophy means thinking. Life is—there is no question of thought. You can simply jump into it.

The ancient pond
a frog jumps in
the sound . . .

Just like that, you can jump into this ancient pond of life. You can know it only by jumping into it. There is no other way to know life. Thinking about it is the surest way to miss it.

A House Divided

You think you know the woman you love. You think you know your husband. You think you know your child. Just because you had carried the child in your womb for nine months, you think you know? You only believe that you know. The child is a mystery; you don't know a thing about the child. The child is as mysterious as the whole existence. You don't know the woman you love. How can you know the woman?—

> Why don't you know your own self?

because you have not yet known yourself. The woman may be close to you, but she can never be so close as you are to yourself.

Hence I say if you don't love yourself, you will not be able to love anybody else in the world. And if you don't know yourself, you will never be able to know anybody else in the world. Love or knowing—it all starts from your own center. The first ripple has to rise there; then it can go on spreading. Then it can go on spreading to the unbounded boundaries of existence. But first it has to start at the very core of your being.

And what is the problem? Why don't you know your own self? This should be the easiest thing in the world, and it has become difficult, the most difficult. It has become almost impossible to know oneself. What has gone wrong? You have the capacity to know. You are there, the capacity to know is there; then what has gone wrong? Why cannot this capacity of knowing turn upon itself?

Only one thing has gone wrong, and unless you put it right, you will remain ignorant of yourself. What has gone wrong is that a split has been created in you. You have lost your integrity. The society has made you into a house divided against yourself. The strategy is simple; once understood, it can be removed. The strategy is that the society has given you ideals for how you should be, and it has enforced those ideals so deeply in you, implanted those ideals so deeply in you, that you are always interested in the ideal—"How I should be?"—and you have forgotten who you are.

You are obsessed with the future ideal, and you have forgotten the present reality. Your eyes are focused on the distant future; hence they cannot turn inward. You are constantly thinking what to do, how to do it, how to be this. Your language has become that of *shoulds* and *oughts*, and the reality consists only of *is*. Reality knows no should, no ought.

A rose flower is a rose flower; there is no question of its being something else. And the lotus is a lotus. Neither the rose ever tries to become a lotus, nor the lotus ever tries to become a rose; hence they are not neurotics. They don't need the psychiatrist; they don't need any psychoanalysis. The rose is healthy because the rose simply lives its reality. And so it is with the whole existence, except human beings. Only human beings have ideals and *should:* "You should be this, that." And then you are divided against your own *is*. *Should* and *is* are enemies.

And you cannot be anything else than you are. Let it sink deep into your heart—you can only be that which you are, never anything else. Once this truth sinks deep, "I can only be myself," all ideals disappear. They are discarded automatically. And when there is no ideal, reality is encountered. Then your eyes are here-now; then you are present to what you are. The division, the split, has disappeared. You are one.

This is the beginning of being one with existence. First be one with yourself. This is the first step of *unio mystica*—be one with yourself. And then the second step, and the last is—be one with existence. The second is easy. The first has become difficult. Because of so much conditioning, so much education, so many civilizing efforts, the first has become difficult.

The First Step

If you have taken the first step—of just accepting yourself and loving yourself as you are, moment to moment . . .

For example, you are sad. This moment you are sad. Your whole conditioning says to you, "You shouldn't be sad. This is bad. You shouldn't be sad; you have to be happy."

Now the division, now the problem. You are sad—that is the truth of this moment. And your conditioning, your mind, says, "You shouldn't be like this; you have to be happy. Smile! What will people think of you?" Your partner may leave you if you are so sad; your friends may desert you if you are so sad; your business will be destroyed if you remain so sad.

You have to laugh; you have to smile; you have to at least pretend that you are happy. If you are a doctor, your patients will not feel good if you are so sad. They want a doctor who is happy, jolly, healthy, and you are looking so sad? Smile! Even if you cannot bring a real smile, bring a false smile, but smile! At least pretend, act.

> If you can live your sadness with no image of being happy, you become happy immediately.

This is the problem: you pretend; you act. A smile you can manage—but you have become two. You have repressed the truth; you have become phony.

And the phony is appreciated by the society. The phony becomes the saint, the phony becomes the great leader, the phony becomes the mahatma, and everybody starts following the phony. The phony is your ideal. That's why you are unable to know yourself. How can you know yourself if you don't accept yourself? You are always repressing your being.

What has to be done then? When you are sad, accept the sadness—this is you. Don't say, "I am sad." Don't say that sadness is something separate from you. Simply say, "I am sadness.

This moment, I am sadness." And live your sadness in total authenticity.

And you will be surprised that a miraculous door opens in your being. If you can live your sadness with no image of being happy, you become happy immediately because the division disappears. There is no division anymore. "I am sadness," and there is no question of any ideal to be anything else. So there is no effort, no conflict.

> All psychological pain exists only because you are divided.

"I am simply this," and there is relaxation. And in that relaxation is grace, and in that relaxation is joy.

All psychological pain exists only because you are divided. Pain means division, and bliss means no division. It will look paradoxical to you that if one is sad and accepts one's sadness, how can one become joyous? It will look paradoxical, but it is so. Try it.

And I am not saying try to be happy; I am not saying, "Accept your sadness so that you can become happy." I am not saying that. If that is your motivation, then nothing will happen; you are still struggling. You will be watching from the corner of your eye. "So much time has passed, and I have accepted even sadness, and I am saying 'I am sadness,' and joy is still not coming." It will not come that way.

Joy is not a goal, it is a by-product. It is a natural consequence of oneness and unity. Just be united with this sadness, for no motivation, for no particular purpose. There is no question of any purpose. This is how you are this moment; this is your truth this moment. And next moment you may be angry—accept that too. And next moment you may be something else—accept that too.

Live moment to moment, with tremendous acceptance, without creating any division, and you are on the way toward self-knowledge. Self-knowledge is not a question of reading the Upanishads and sitting silently and reciting, "Aham brahmasmi, I am God." These are all foolish efforts. Either you know you are godly or you don't know it. You can go on for your whole life repeating, "Aham brahmasmi, I am God." You can waste your whole life in repeating it; you will not know it.

If you know it, there is no point in repeating it. Why are you repeating it? If you know, you know. If you don't know, how can you know by repetition? Just see the whole stupidity of it. But that's what is being done in this country and in other countries also, in monasteries and ashrams. What are people doing?— parrot-like repetition.

I am giving you a totally different approach. It is not by repetition of the Koran or Bible or Vedas that you will become a knower—no. You will only become knowledgeable. Then how does one come to know oneself?—drop the division. The division is the whole problem. You are against yourself.

Drop all ideals that create this antagonism in you. You are the way you are—accept it with joy, with gratitude. And

> You are the way you are—accept it with joy, with gratitude. And suddenly a harmony will be felt.

suddenly a harmony will be felt: the two selves in you, the ideal self and the real self, will not be there to fight anymore. They will merge and meet into one.

It is not really sadness that gives you pain. It is the interpretation that sadness is *wrong* that gives you pain, that becomes a psychological problem. It is not anger that is painful; it is the idea that anger is *wrong* that creates psychological anxiety. It is the interpretation, not the fact. The fact is always liberating.

Be the Truth That You Are

Jesus says, "Truth liberates." And that is of tremendous import— yes, truth liberates, but not "knowing about" truth. *Be* the truth, and it liberates; be the truth, and there is liberation. You need not bring it, you need not wait for it; it happens instantly.

How to be the truth? You already are the truth. You are carrying false ideals; they are creating the trouble. Drop the ideals. For a few days, be a natural being, just as the trees and animals and birds. Accept your being as you are, and a great silence arises. How can it be otherwise? There is no interpretation. Then sadness is beautiful; it has depth. Then anger is also beautiful; it has life, vitality. Then sex too is beautiful because it has creativity. When there is no interpretation, all is beautiful. When all is beautiful, you are relaxed. In that relaxation you have fallen into your own source, and that brings self-knowledge.

Falling into one's own source is what is meant by "Know thyself." It is not a question of knowledge, it is a question of inner transformation. And what transformation am I talking about? I am not giving you any ideal that you have to be like; I am not saying that you have to transform from what you are and become somebody else. You have simply to relax into whatsoever you are and just see.

Have you heard what I am saying? Just see the point—it is liberating. And a great harmony, a great music is heard. That music is of self-knowledge. And your life starts changing. Then you have a magic key which unlocks all the locks.

If you accept sadness, sadness will disappear. How long can you be sad if you accept sadness? If you are capable of accepting sadness, you will be capable of absorbing it in your being; it will become your depth. And how long will you be able to be angry if you accept anger? Anger feeds on rejection. If you accept it, you have absorbed the energy.

And anger has great energy in it, vitality, and when that energy is absorbed, you become more vital. Your life then has a passion to it; it is a flame. It is not a dull, insipid life; it has intelligence and passion and sharpness. And if you have accepted sex, one day sex disappears too. And it releases great creativity in you because sex is the potential of creativity. And then you become a creator. Great paintings may arise through you; great poetry may come. Great songs may be born, or music. Anything and everything is possible then—you participate with existence.

Sex is the lowest form of creativity, just the seed of creativity. Once the seed has broken, has dissolved, has been absorbed, your whole being becomes creative. And to be creative is to be blissful; to be creative is to be one with God. When you become a creator, you participate in God.

And I am not saying that unless you paint and write poetry you will not be a creator. Buddha didn't paint, has not written any poetry, but his whole life was of creativity. Whosoever he touched was transformed. Whosoever was courageous enough to come close to him was reborn. He created a great energy field, a buddhafield, and whosoever entered in that field was never the same again. That is his creativity.

He didn't write any visible poetry, but the way he walks is poetry, the way he looks at people is poetry. He never danced. But if you watch, silently sitting underneath the bodhi tree, there is a great dance happening in him. It is an invisible dance; it is subtle, it is not gross. It is not of the physical; it is a spiritual dance. He is not separate from existence. He is dancing in the trees in the wind and he is dancing with the stars and he is dancing with the whole. He is not separate anymore.

Do you understand the difference? If you try to drop sex, all creativity will disappear from your life. That's what happened in the unfortunate country of India. People tried to drop sex; people tried to somehow impose celibacy on themselves. And they all became uncreative; they all became dull; they lost intelligence. You can go around and see Indian mahatmas, and you will not see such dull and stupid people anywhere else in the world. Their whole life consists of living in a very uncreative way.

And they are praised for uncreative things. Somebody fasts, that's why he is praised—not for any dance. Somebody sleeps on a bed of thorns, that's why he is praised. Now, he has not done anything creative in the world. He has not made the world a little more beautiful than he found it. He will leave the world as ugly as it was before or even uglier. But he is praised because he lies on a bed of thorns. What is the point of it?

If you repress sex, creativity disappears. If you accept sex, sex is transformed into creativity. If you accept anger, it releases great vitality and passion in you. Your life becomes a passionate life. Then it is a life of involvement, commitment, participation. Then you are not just a spectator. Then you are in the thick of it, the dance of life, part of it—you are involved each moment. Then you are not an escapist. You live joyously and totally. Then you contribute something to existence; then you are not futile; then you have some meaning. But anger has to be accepted. Then the anger's energy is absorbed.

Whenever you reject something, you have rejected some energy. You have said, "I don't want to absorb this energy." But this is *your* energy, and the rejected energy will keep you poor. Reject anger, and you have rejected the possibility of being vital; now you will be dull. Reject sex, and you have rejected the possibility of being creative; now no poetry, no song, no dance is going to happen in your life. You will just be a dead man walking; your life will be an empty gesture, impotent.

If you have rejected sadness, then you will not have any depth; you will remain shallow. Your laughter will also be shallow because it will not have any depth. That sadness can only be released through acceptance; your laughter will be just on the surface. That's what I mean when I see people and call them phony. A phony person is one who is only pretending to live but not really living, is afraid of life. And this phoniness comes through rejection. Go on rejecting everything—keep an ideal in the mind that you have to become a Buddha, that you have to become a Jesus—and you will never become one. On the contrary, you will lose all possibility of ever becoming anything. Forget all about Buddhas and Krishnas and Christs; they are not ideals to be imitated. Don't have any ideals; be a destroyer of ideals. This is rebellion, and this is religion too.

When there are no ideals haunting you, torturing you, you fall into harmony with yourself. And when you don't reject anything, all energies are yours; you are enriched. Then you have tremendous energy. And that tremendous energy is joy; that energy is delight. And falling into your own source, you become a knower.

And the moment you know yourself, you have known all, because it is the same. That which is in me is in everybody. Only forms are different, houses are different. It is the same consciousness. That in me which says, "I am," also says the same in you: "I am." This I-am-ness is one—it is the same in the trees, unspoken; it is the same in the rocks, fast asleep, but it is the same I-am-ness. And to know this is to know the meaning of *Aham brahmasmi*, "I am God."

The Secret Key

You know only your hands and feet; this is your abode, this is your house. You are acquainted only with the temple—when are you going to be acquainted with the deity of the temple? Who is this who lives in this house? Who is embodied in the body? What is this consciousness?

If you are listening to me, you are listening through the ears; if you are seeing me, you are seeing through the eyes—certainly you are not the ears, and you are not the eyes. The eyes and ears are windows—somebody is hidden behind, standing behind the windows.

Just watch—your eyes are windows. When you are looking at me, you are looking through the eyes. But who are you? Who is this who is looking at me? Who is this who is hearing? What is this consciousness?

Don't reject anything; otherwise you will never be able to know this consciousness. Accept all that you are. If you reject anything, you recoil from your own energies, you create

> Relaxed, serene, utterly at home—this is the destined home.

fragments. Don't recoil from your energies. When anger is there, accept it. When sadness is there, accept it. This is your energy; this is the gift of existence. Absorb it; digest it. It is you.

And when you are not recoiling from anything, when you don't have any interpretations of good and bad, when you don't condemn anything—when you forget all about judgment, when you are not a constant judger, assessor, condemner, evaluator, when all these things have disappeared, and you are simply a tremendous acceptance of all that is—knowing happens. And in that knowing, godliness is known.

Be the truth that you are, and you will be liberated; you will be liberated from all illusions, from all mirages. Be the truth, each moment, that you are. This is the message of all the Buddhas—be the truth each moment that you are. Don't hanker for anything else; don't desire for anything else. Don't try to become, just be the moment you are. Relaxed, serene, utterly at home—this is the destined home.

This is the home you have been searching for so many lives. But your very methodology of search has been wrong. You had made it a goal, and it is not a goal; it is the source. God is not where we are going, God is from where we are coming. God is not there, God is here. God is not then, God is now.

Accept yourself in tremendous gratitude—whatsoever is, is, and it can't be otherwise, so don't fight with it.

No fact ever creates any psychological pain. It is the interpretation that brings pain to you. Pain is your creation because it is your interpretation. Change the interpretation and the same fact becomes pleasant. Drop all interpretations and the fact is simply a fact, neither painful nor pleasant. Don't choose; don't have any preferences. Just be watchful, accepting and watchful, and you have the secret key in your hands.

The Fear of Finding Yourself

A friend has asked, "Why am I scared to accept myself the way I am?" Everybody is in the same situation. Everybody is scared to accept himself the way he is. This is how all the past centuries of mankind have cultivated, conditioned every child, every human being.

The strategy is simple but very dangerous. The strategy is to condemn you and to give you ideals so that you are always trying to become someone else. The Christian is trying to become a Jesus; the Buddhist is trying to become a Buddha. To distract you from yourself seems so clever a device that perhaps the people who have been doing it are themselves unaware of it.

> Everybody is scared to accept himself the way he is.

What Jesus said on the cross—his last words to humanity—is immensely significant in many ways, particularly in this context.

He prayed to God, "Father, forgive these people because they know not what they are doing."

This is applicable to every father and to every mother, to every teacher and every priest and every moralist; to the people who manage culture, society, civilization, and who try to mold every individual in a certain way. Perhaps they also don't know what they are doing. Perhaps they think they are doing everything for your good. I don't suspect their intentions, but I certainly want you to be aware that they are ignorant; they are unconscious people.

A small child is born into the hands of an unconscious society. And the unconscious society starts molding the child according to its own ideals, forgetting the one thing which is the most fundamental: that the child has a potential of his own. He has to grow—not into a Jesus or into a Krishna or into a Buddha—he has to grow to be himself.

If the child misses growing into being himself, he will remain utterly miserable his whole life. His life will become just a hell and a curse, and he will not know what has gone wrong. He has been put in the wrong direction from the very beginning. And he thinks the people who have put him in the wrong direction love him, are his benefactors. Actually they are his greatest enemies. The parents, the teachers, the priests, and the leaders of the society are the greatest enemies of every individual who has been born on the earth up to now. Without being aware, they are distracting you from yourself.

And to distract you, you have to be absolutely conditioned

about one thing: that you are unworthy, undeserving, of no use at all as you are. Of course you can become worthy of respect, dignity, if you follow the rules and regulations given to you by others. If you are able to manage to be a hypocrite, you will be a prestigious citizen of the society. But if you insist on being sincere, honest, authentic, yourself, you will be condemned by everybody.

And it needs tremendous courage to be condemned by everybody. It needs a steel spine to stand on your own and declare: "I am not going to be anybody else but myself. Good or bad, acceptable or not acceptable, prestigious or not prestigious, one thing is certain—that I can be only myself and nobody else." This needs a tremendously revolutionary approach toward life. This is the basic revolt that each individual needs if he wants ever to be out of the vicious circle of misery.

You are asking me: "Why am I scared to accept myself the way I am?" Because you have not been accepted by anyone the way you are. They have created the fear and the apprehension that if you accept yourself, you will be rejected by everybody.

This is an absolute condition of every society and every culture that has existed up to now: that either you accept yourself and be rejected by all, or you reject yourself and gain the respect and honor of your whole society and culture. The choice is really very difficult. Obviously the majority is going to choose respectability. But with respectability come all kinds of anxieties, anguishes: a meaninglessness, a desert-like life where nothing grows, where nothing is green, where no flower ever blossoms, where you will walk and walk and walk and you will never even find an oasis.

I am reminded of Leo Tolstoy. He used to have a dream that psychoanalysts of different schools have been interpreting for almost a whole century. The dream was very strange, but not to me. To me it needs no psychoanalysis, but simple common sense. The dream was repeated every night continuously for years. It was strangely nightmarish, and Tolstoy awoke in the middle of every night, perspiring, although there was no danger in the dream.

But if you can understand the meaninglessness of the dream . . . That was the problem that became the nightmare. This dream represents almost everybody's life. No psychoanalytic school has been able to figure out what kind of dream it is because there is no parallel; it is unprecedented.

The dream used to be the same every night. A vast desert, as far as you can see just desert and desert, and two boots, which Tolstoy recognized as his, go on walking. But he is missing; just the boots go on making noise in the sand. And it continues because the desert is endless. They never reach anywhere. Behind he can see the prints of the boots for miles, and ahead he can see the boots going on walking.

Ordinarily you will not think it is a nightmare. But if you think a little more closely: every day, every night the same dream of utter futility, reaching nowhere. There seems to be no destiny, and nobody is in the boots—they are empty.

He told all the well-known psychoanalysts of his day in Russia. Nobody could figure out what it meant because there is no book that describes any dream which can even be called a little bit similar to this. It is absolutely unique. But to me there is no question of any psychoanalysis. It is a simple dream representing every human being's life. You are walking in a desert because you are not walking toward the goal that is intrinsic in your being. You are not going to reach anywhere. The more you go away, the more you will be going away from yourself. And the more you look for any meaning, the more you will find utter emptiness and nothing else. That is the meaning. The man is missing; only the boots are walking.

You are not in what you are doing. You are not in what you are being. You are not in what you are pretending. It is utter hollowness, pure hypocrisy.

But the way it has been created is a simple method: tell everybody, "As you are, you are absolutely undeserving—even to exist. As you are, you are just ugly, an accident. As you are, you should be ashamed of yourself because you don't have anything worthy of honor and respect." Naturally, every child starts doing things that are supposed to be honorable. He goes on becoming more and more false, more and more phony, more and more distant from his authentic reality, his very being—and then the fear arises.

Whenever a longing is felt to know yourself, it is immediately followed by great fear. The fear is that if you find yourself, you are going to lose respect for yourself—even in your own eyes.

The society is too heavy on every individual. It makes every effort to condition you so heavily that you start thinking that you are the conditioning—and you become part of the society, against your own being. You become a Christian, you become a

Hindu, you become a Mohammedan, and you forget completely that you were born just as a human being, with no religion, with no politics, with no nation, with no race. You were born just a pure possibility of growth.

According to me, to become a seeker is to bring yourself back to yourself, whatsoever the consequences, whatsoever the risk. You have to come back to yourself. You may not find a Jesus there. There is no need: one Jesus is enough. You may not find a Gautam Buddha. It is perfectly okay because too many Gautam Buddhas in existence will be simply boring. Existence does not want to repeat people. It is so creative that it always brings something new in each individual, a new potential, a new possibility, a new height, a new dimension, a new peak. To become a seeker is a revolt against all societies and all cultures and all civilizations for the simple reason that they are against the individual.

I am absolutely for the individual. I can sacrifice every society and every religion and every civilization—the whole history of mankind—just for a single individual. The individual is the most valuable phenomenon because the individual is part of existence.

You will have to drop your fear. It has been imposed on you; it is not natural. Watch every small child: he accepts himself perfectly; there is no condemnation, there is no desire to be anybody else. But everybody, as he grows, is distracted. You will have to gather courage to come back to yourself. The whole society will prevent you; you will be condemned. But it is far better to be condemned by the whole world than to remain miserable and phony and false and live a life of somebody else.

You can have a blissful life, and there are not two ways, only one single way. You have just to be yourself, whatever you are. From there, from that deep acceptance and respect for yourself, you will start growing. You will bring flowers of your own—not Christian, not Buddhist, not Hindu—just absolutely your own, a new contribution to existence.

But it needs immense courage to go alone on a path leaving the whole crowd on the highway. To be in the crowd, one feels cozy, warm; to go alone, naturally one feels afraid. The mind goes on arguing within that "the whole of humanity cannot be wrong, and I am going alone. It is better just to be part of the crowd because then

> It needs immense courage to go alone on a path leaving the whole crowd on the highway.

you are not responsible if things go wrong." Everybody is responsible.

The moment you depart from the crowd you are taking your responsibility in your own hands. If something goes wrong, you are responsible.

But remember one very fundamental thing: responsibility is one side of the coin, and the other side is freedom. You can have both together, or you can drop both together. If you don't want to have responsibility, you cannot have freedom, and without freedom there is no growth.

So you have to accept responsibility for yourself, and you have to live in absolute freedom so that you can grow, whatever you are. You may turn out to be a rosebush; you may turn out to be just a marigold flower; you may turn out just to be a wildflower that has no name. But one thing is certain: whatever you turn out to be, you will be immensely happy. You will be utterly blissful.

You Are Incomparable

People are continuously comparing themselves with others. They become happy, they become unhappy because of the comparisons.

I had a meeting with a very famous Hindu saint. He told a few other people who had gathered to listen to what transpired between us: "The secret of happiness is always to look to those who are unhappy. Look at the crippled, and you will feel happy that you are not crippled. Look at the blind, and you will feel happy that you are not blind. Look at the poor, and you will feel happy that you are not poor."

I had to stop this idiot! I said, "You don't understand a simple fact. Once a person starts comparing, he cannot stop at only comparing with those who are unfortunate. He will also look at those who are richer than him, who are more beautiful than him, who are stronger than him, who are more respectable than him. Then he will be miserable. You are not giving him the secret of happiness; you are giving him the secret of being in absolute misery."

It has been taught down the ages in almost all the religious scriptures, in different words, but the essential secret is the same: feel contented because there are people who are so miserable. Thank God that you are not so miserable. But this cannot remain one-sided. Once you learn the way of comparison, you cannot compare yourself only with those who are inferior to you. Inevitably you will also have to compare yourself with those who are superior to you—and then there will be immense misery.

In fact, comparison is not the right thing to do. You are yourself, and there is nobody else with whom you can be compared.

You are incomparable. So is the other person. Never compare.

Comparison is one of the causes that is keeping you tethered to the mundane—because comparison creates competition, comparison creates ambition. It does not come alone; it brings all its companions with it. And once you become competitive, there is no end to it; you will end before it does. Once you become ambitious, you have chosen the most stupid path for your life.

Henry Ford was once asked . . . And he seems to be one of the wisest men of this century because his small statements make so much sense. He was the first man to say that "history is bunk," and that is absolutely true.

He was asked, "What have you learned through your successful life?" He was one of the most successful men you can conceive of; from poverty he rose to be the richest man in the world. What he said has to be remembered.

Henry Ford said, "Through all my successful life I have learned only one thing: I have learned to climb staircases, to climb ladders. And then when I reach the last rung of the ladder, I feel so stupid and so embarrassed because there is no longer anywhere to go.

"And I cannot say to the people who are behind me, struggling hard to reach the same ladder where I am feeling stupid, what I have been struggling for. And nobody will listen to me if

I say to them, 'Stop wherever you are. Don't waste time because there is nothing. Once you reach the top, you are stuck. You cannot get down because that looks like falling back. You cannot go ahead because there is nowhere to go ahead.'"

The presidents and prime ministers of countries just feel stuck. Now they know there is only one thing that can happen, and that is the fall. There is nothing to rise to; there is nowhere to go except to fall from the place that they have reached. So they cling to their seats.

But this is not the right kind of life. First you go on climbing ladders, struggling with people; then ultimately you are stuck and you cling to the last rung so that nobody can take you away from it. Is this a madhouse?

Man has turned this planet into a madhouse. If you want to be sane, first be yourself—without any guilt, without any condemnation. Accept yourself with humbleness and simplicity.

This is a gift of existence to you. Feel grateful, and start searching for what can help you to grow as you are—not to become a carbon copy of somebody else, but just to remain your original self.

Every Truth Is Individual

A story from Chuang Tzu:

Symphony for a Seabird

You cannot put a big load in a small bag, nor can you, with a short rope, draw water from a deep well . . .

Have you not heard how a bird from the sea was blown in-
shore and landed outside the capital of Lu?
The prince ordered a solemn reception, offered the seabird
wine in the Sacred Precinct, called for musicians to play
compositions of Shun, slaughtered cattle to nourish it.
Dazed with symphonies, the unhappy seabird died of despair.
How should you treat a bird? As yourself or as a bird?
Ought not a bird nest in deep woodland or fly
over meadow and marsh?
Ought it not swim on river and pond, feed on eels
and fish, fly in formation with other fowl,
and rest in the reeds?
Bad enough for a seabird to be surrounded by men
and frightened by their voices! That was not enough!
They killed it with music.
Water is for fish, air for men.
Natures differ, and needs with them.
Hence the wise men of old did not lay down
one measure for all.

There is no human nature as such; there are human natures. Each individual is a universe unto himself; you cannot make any general rules. All general rules become false. This has to be remembered very deeply because on the path there is every possibility you may start following rules, and once you become a victim of rules, you will never come to know who you are.

You can know yourself only in total freedom, and rules are prisons. They are prisons because no one can make rules for you;

he may have discovered the truth through those rules, but they were for him. Nature differs. They helped him; they will not help you; on the contrary, they will hinder you.

So let understanding be the only rule. Learn, grow in understanding, but don't follow rules. Rules are dead; understanding is alive. Rules will become an imprisonment; understanding will give you the infinite sky.

> Learn, grow in understanding, but don't follow rules. Rules are dead; understanding is alive.

Now we will enter the story:

You cannot put a big load in a small bag, nor can you, with a short rope, draw water from a deep well . . .

This is what everybody is doing, trying to put a big load in a small bag. You never bother about the bag, what your capacity is. The first thing is to know your limitations, then to think about your achievement. What is your capacity? What are you capable of? What is your intrinsic capacity? Nobody bothers about it. If a man who has no musical ear goes on trying to become a musician, his whole life will be wasted, because a musician is born, not made.

A man who has no feeling goes on trying to become a poet or a painter. A man who has no eyes who tries to become a painter is going to be a failure, because a painter has a different type of eye—almost the third eye. When you look at the trees, you see one green; when a painter looks, he sees thousands of greens, not one. Each tree has a greenery of its own. He feels color; color has a vibration for him; the whole world is nothing but color.

Hindus say that the whole world is sound. It happened that those few people who wrote the Upanishads were poets, musicians; they had an ear for sound. Then the whole universe turned into a sound—*omkar, anahata*. If a man who has never been in love with music goes on trying with the mantra *aum*, nothing happens. He goes on repeating it inside; nothing happens. He goes to this master and that, and never thinks about his own capacity.

If you have a musical ear, if you have a heart which can understand music—not only understand, but feel—then a mantra will be helpful. Then inner sound and you can become one; then you can move with that sound to subtler and subtler layers. Then a moment comes when all sounds stop and only the universal sound remains. That is *aum*. That is why Hindus say the whole world consists of sound. This is not true, not an absolute truth; this is the truth of the musician.

Remember: there are no absolute truths, every truth is individual—it is your truth. There is no truth as objectivity. Your truth may not be a truth to me; my truth may not be a truth to you because truth is not objective. I am there, involved in it; my truth means me, your truth means you.

When Buddha reaches, when Jesus or Chuang Tzu reach, they have reached the same universal source, but their interpretation differs. A Buddha is not a musician at all; he finds no sound there. He is not a painter; he finds no color there. He is a very silent man; silence is his music. That is why he finds a formless void, *shunya*, everything empty. That is his truth. He has come to the same source. The source is one, but the persons who come are different. They look, they see, they feel in different ways. That is why there are so many philosophies, so many religions.

When Meera comes to the same source, she starts dancing. You cannot conceive of Buddha dancing; you cannot conceive of Jesus dancing! Meera starts dancing; she has come to the beloved. The heart of a woman, the heart, the feeling of love—then the source becomes the beloved. She has come to her lover. The source is the same, the truth ultimately is the same, but the moment someone says it, it is different. And remember, nobody's truth can be yours; you have to uncover it.

The first thing is to remember your capacity. You can reach only in a certain way; you can reach only through you.

You cannot put a big load in a small bag, nor can you, with a short rope, draw water from a deep well . . . Know your capacity; that is the first point. If you know your capacity rightly, then the first step has been taken, and the last is not very far away. If the first is wrong, then you may walk and walk for lives together, and you will not reach anywhere.

Have you not heard how a bird from the sea was blown inshore and landed outside the capital of Lu?

A beautiful parable; a bird from the sea landed outside the capital of Lu, a beautiful bird.

The prince ordered a solemn reception . . . Because a prince is a prince, and he thought a really princely bird has come. The bird was so beautiful that he had to be received as other princes have to be received. But how to receive a bird? The prince had his own ways. He received the bird . . .

. . . he ordered a solemn reception, offered the seabird wine in the Sacred Precinct, called for musicians to play the compositions of Shun, slaughtered cattle to nourish it. Dazed with symphonies, the unhappy seabird died of despair.

Everything was done to receive the guest, but nobody bothered who this guest was. The guest was received according to the host, not according to the guest—and that killed the poor bird. Many of you are simply dead because of the host. Nobody looks at you. A child is born and the parents start thinking what to make of him. Even before he is born they start thinking.

I was staying in the home of a friend. The friend is a professor in a university; his wife is also a professor. Both are very intelligent persons with gold medals and certificates and PhDs. I saw their daughter—they have only one daughter—playing on the piano, weeping and crying. So I asked the mother, "What is the matter?"

The mother said, "I always wanted to be a musician, and my parents wouldn't allow it. Now this is not going to happen again to my daughter; she has to be a musician. I have suffered so much; my parents wouldn't allow, they forced me to be a professor. I am not going to force my daughter to be a professor; she is going to be a musician." And the daughter was crying and weeping.

You are so confused because of others: your mother wants you to be something, your father something else. It is bound to be so because they never agree; fathers and mothers never agree.

Mulla Nasruddin's son told me, "I would like to be a doctor, but my mother insists, 'You have to be an engineer.' So what to do?"

I said, "Do one thing; spread the rumor that your father wants you to be an engineer." So now he is a doctor!

They are always opposed, father and mother, and their opposition goes deep within you. It becomes an inner conflict. Your father and your mother may be dead, no longer in this world, but they are within your unconscious, still fighting. They will never leave you in peace. Whatsoever you do, your father says do it, then your mother says don't. Your inner conflict is your parents' conflict. Then there are uncles and brothers and sisters and so many relatives, and you alone amid so many well-wishers. They all want you to be something according to them. They destroy you. Then the whole life becomes a confusion; you don't know what you want to be; you don't know where you want to go; you don't know what you are doing and why you are doing it. Then you feel miserable. Misery comes into being if you cannot grow to be a natural being, if you cannot grow according to you.

That happened to that seabird, and this has happened to all seabirds: you are all seabirds. One day you landed in a womb in the capital of Lu; you were received with great pomp and show. Astrologers decided what was to be done; musicians welcomed with their music; parents with their love. And all together they have just made you insane and nothing else.

A wise man receives you not according to him; he receives you according to you. A seabird was killed by the musicians and their beautiful symphonies—and the prince was doing everything right! That was how a guest had to be received.

How should you treat a seabird? As yourself or as a bird?

Always give an opportunity to the other to be himself; that is what understanding is, that is what love is. Don't force yourself on others. Your wishes may be good, but the result will be bad. A good wish is not enough in itself. It may turn poisonous. The real point is not your good wish; the real point is to give freedom to the other to be himself or herself. Allow your wife to be herself, allow your husband to be himself, allow your child to be himself—don't force.

We are all seabirds, unknown to each other, strangers. Nobody knows who you are. At the most, all we can do is to help you to be whatsoever you are going to be. And the future is unknown; it cannot be forced. There is no way to know it. No astrology is going to help; these are all foolish methods. They depend on stupid people. They continue because we go on asking to know about the future so that we can plan.

> A good wish is not enough in itself. It may turn poisonous.

Life cannot be planned; it is an unplanned flood. It is good that it is unplanned. If it is planned, then everything will be dead and boring. It is good that nobody is able to predict the future; it is good that the future remains unknown, unpredictable, because there lies the whole freedom. If the future becomes known, then there is no freedom left. Then you will move like a predictable mechanism. But that is what we want, or that is what we try to do.

If you are a little understanding, give others around you freedom to be themselves, and don't allow anybody to interfere with your freedom. Don't make anybody a slave to you, and don't become a slave to anybody. This is what sannyas is. This is my meaning of sannyas—one who has decided not to enslave anybody and not to be enslaved by anybody; one who has decided to remain authentically true to himself. Wheresoever this truth leads, he is ready to go.

This is courage. It may lead you into insecurity; if you would like to be more secure, then you will listen to others and their well-wishing, and then their symphonies will kill you. They have already killed you. Why do you listen to others?—because you feel they know more.

I have heard a small child talking to his elder brother—the small one was five and the elder was ten—the junior was saying to the senior, "Go to mother and ask for her permission so that we can go to the theater."

The senior said, "Why not you? Why don't you go?"

The junior said, "You have known her longer than me."

This is the whole problem: you listen to your mother because she has known this world longer than you, your father because he has known longer than you. But do you think anybody knows anything just by being here for long? Do you think time gives understanding? Do you think seniority is wisdom? Then go to the government offices and look at the senior people there. Seniority may be wisdom in a government office; it is not in life.

Life is not understood through time, it is understood through meditation. It is a going inward. Time is an outer movement; time is on the periphery. A man can live for a thousand years and remain stupid. He will become really more stupid because he will grow. If you have the seed of stupidity in you, within a thousand years you will become such a vast tree that millions of stupid people can rest under you. Whatsoever you have grows; nothing is static, everything is growing. So a stupid person becomes more stupid, a wise person becomes more wise—but time has nothing to do with understanding.

Understanding is not temporal; it is not more experience. It is not the quantity of experience that makes you wise, it is the quality. A single experience can give you the kind of wisdom that many lives may not give you if you bring the quality of awareness to the experience. A man may have made love to many women, thousands of women, thousands of times. Do you think he knows what love is? There is quantity—ask a Byron, any Don Juan; there is quantity! Don Juans keep records; they go on counting how many women they have conquered. There is quantity, but have they known love?

A single love can give you wisdom if you bring quality to it. The quality has to be brought by you. What is that quality? That quality is awareness. If you make love to a single woman for a single time with your total being, fully alert, you have come to know what love is. Otherwise you can go on and on and on, it becomes a repetition. And then you need not do anything; the wheel repeats by itself, it becomes automatic.

Wisdom is something that happens when you bring awareness

to any experience. The meeting of awareness and experience is wisdom. Experience plus awareness is wisdom. With experience plus more experience, plus more experience—then quantity is gained, but there is no quality which makes you free and knowing.

Whenever a child is born, if the mother loves the child, if the father loves the child, they will not force themselves on him, because they should know at least this much: they have been failures, so why give the same pattern to this child? Why destroy another life again? But look at the stupidity. They would like the child to just follow their path. They have reached nowhere, and they know deep down they are empty, hollow, and they are forcing a child to move again on the same path, to reach to the same hollowness in the end. Why?—because it feels good to the ego to know "My child is following me."

You may not have reached anywhere, but your son following you gives you a good feeling. As if you have attained, and that is why the son is following you. If you are not satisfied by a son, then you can gather followers, disciples. There are many who are always ready to fall into anybody's trap because people are so unfulfilled, they are ready to follow anybody's advice. The problem is, they are unfulfilled because of others' advice—and they go on asking for it again and again.

Mind is a vicious thing. You are so empty, hollow, because you have been following others' advice, and again you are in search of others to advise you? When will you become aware that basically you are missing because you have not followed your inner voice?

A master cannot give you rules. If a master gives you rules, know well he is a pseudo master. Escape from him! A master can only give you understanding, how to understand yourself. Then rules will come, but they will come out of your understanding.

How would you treat a seabird? As yourself or as a bird?
Ought not a bird nest in deep woodland or fly
over meadow and marsh?
Ought it not swim on river and pond, feed on eels
and fish, fly in formation with other fowls,
and rest in the reeds?
Bad enough for a seabird to be surrounded by men
and frightened by their voices. That was not enough!
They killed it with music.

Everybody is being killed by music. That music comes out of well-wishers, good wishing, the do-gooders. The whole thing seems to be so absurd and insane. If you plant one thousand trees, and only one comes to flower and nine hundred and ninety-nine die, will anybody call you a gardener? Will anybody give you any credit for the one tree that has flowered? They will say it must have flowered in spite of you, because you killed nine hundred and ninety-nine. You cannot take credit for the one; it must have escaped somehow. It must have escaped your skill, your experience, your wisdom.

In millions of people, one becomes a Buddha and flowers. What is happening? Why do many trees have to live without flowers? Look at a tree when there are no flowers and flowers never come, what sadness settles on the tree. It cannot laugh; it cannot sing; it cannot dance. Flowers are needed to dance. How can you dance? Even if I say to you, "Dance!" how can you dance? Dance is an overflowing delight, so overflowing that every cell of the body starts dancing; you become a dancing cosmos. But how?—energy is not flowing, there is no energy coming. You are somehow carrying yourself, dragging yourself. How can you dance? Flowers come when the tree has so much that it can give; flowers are a gift. It is a sharing; it is saying to the whole universe, "I am more than I need." It is a song. The tree is saying, "Now I move into the world of luxury, my needs are fulfilled." The tree has more than it needs, then flowering happens.

You are so discontented, you don't have even as much as you need. How can you dance? How can you sing? How can you meditate?

Meditation is the ultimate flowering, the ecstasy that comes only when you are overflowing in a flood; when you have so much energy that you cannot sit, you can only dance; when you have so much energy you cannot do anything but share, invite guests to share your energy and your delight, your singing and your dancing.

What has happened to man? What has man done to man that nobody flowers? If Buddha flowers, remember well it is not because of you, it is in spite of you. It is in spite of Buddha's father and mother, in spite of his teachers.

It happened:

One of my university teachers came to see me. He said, "You must remember that I was your teacher."

I told him, "Yes, I remember. How can I forget? It is in spite of you that I am whatsoever I am. You could not succeed with me. You tried, and I will always feel thankful toward you that you failed. You couldn't succeed!"

He really loved me, and he tried every way to force me into the academic world. He loved me so much, and he cared so much about me that whenever there would be an examination, in the morning he would come with his car and take me to the examination hall because he was always afraid I may not go, or I may be meditating. Before examinations he would come to tell me, "Read this, read this, read this. It is coming; I am the paper-setter." Again and again he would remind me, "Have you read that or not? And know well: I am the paper-setter and it is coming"—because he was always afraid I wouldn't listen to him.

He loved me. Your parents also loved you, your teachers also loved you, but they are unconscious, they don't know what they are doing. Even if they love, something goes wrong. That is, they try to give you something according to themselves. He wanted me to become a great university professor, somewhere in some great university, head of a department or a dean or a vice-chancellor.

He imagined, and I always laughed and asked him, "But what will I gain through this? What have you gained? You are the head of a department, a dean with so many degrees, Honorary Doctor of Literature and this and that; what have you gained?"

He would smile knowingly and say, "You just wait and do whatsoever I am saying." Because at this question, "What have you gained?" he would always feel a little perplexed, confused—what to say?

> You cannot be treated as things. Things can be similar; souls cannot be.

He had not gained anything, and now he was nearing death. He would have liked his ambition to move through me. He would have liked me to carry his ambition.

A father dies unfulfilled; he hopes that at least his son will reach to the goal. This is how it goes on and on; nobody reaches.

Love is not enough. Awareness is needed. If love is there without awareness, it becomes an imprisonment. If love is there with awareness, it becomes a freedom. It helps you to be yourself.

Bad enough for a seabird to be surrounded by men and frightened by their voices.

That was not enough! They killed it with music.

Water is for fish and air for man.

Natures differ and needs with them.

Hence the wise men of old did not lay down one measure for all.

You cannot be treated as things. Things can be similar; souls cannot be. You can have one million Ford cars just the same. You can replace one Ford car with another Ford car and there will be no trouble, but you cannot replace a human being. When a human being disappears, the place that he occupied will always remain forever and forever unoccupied. Nobody can occupy it; it is impossible to occupy it because nobody can be exactly the same as that man was. Everybody is unique, so no rules can be laid down.

. . . the wise men of old . . . But if you go to the wise men of today, you will find rules and regulations and everything: a framework. They will make you a soldier but not a seeker. A soldier is a dead man because his whole function is to bring death in the world. He cannot be allowed to be very alive, otherwise how will he bring death? Death can only come through a dead man. He has to kill. Before he kills others, he himself has to be killed completely, through rules. The whole training in the army is to kill the aliveness of the person, the consciousness of the person, make him an automaton. They go on saying to him, "Right turn, left turn, right turn, left turn," for years together, every day for hours! What nonsense is going on? Why "right turn," why "left turn"? There is a point in it; they want to make you an automaton. "Right turn"—and every day for hours you are doing it. It becomes a bodily phenomenon. When they say "Right turn!" you need not think about it—the body simply moves. When they say "Left turn!" the body simply moves. Now you are a mechanism. And when they say "Shoot!" you shoot. The body moves; the consciousness does not interfere.

The whole training of armies all over the world is to cut consciousness from your actions so actions become automatic; you become more efficient, skilled—because consciousness is always a trouble. If you are killing a person and you think, you will miss. If you think, "Why kill this man? He has not done anything to me. I don't even know who he is; he is a stranger . . ." If you think, you will also have the feeling that you have a mother at home, a wife, a small child waiting for you, and the same is going to be the case with the other. A mother must be waiting somewhere, a wife praying that the husband will come back, a child hoping that his father will be back. Why kill this man and kill those hopes of a child, of a wife, of a mother, of a father, brother, friends? Why kill this man? And he has not done anything wrong to you . . . Two politicians have gone mad; they can go and fight with each other and decide the matter. Why decide through others?

If you are alert, aware, it will be impossible for you to shoot and kill. The whole training of the army is how to divide awareness and action, how to cut and create a gap. So awareness continues on its own and action continues on its own and they become parallel; they never meet.

Just the opposite is the training of a seeker of truth: how to destroy the gap that exists between consciousness and action, how to bring them together. They should not be parallel lines; they should become one whole. It is how to be conscious in each of your actions, how not to be an automaton. When all your automatism disappears, you have become enlightened; then you are a Buddha.

> Dropping the rules does not mean that you become anti-social.

Through rules this cannot be done. Through rules you can be made a soldier, but you cannot be made a seeker. All rules have to be dropped; understanding has to be gained. But remember, dropping the rules does not mean that you become anti-social. Dropping the rules only means that because you exist in the society you follow certain rules, but they are just rules of the game, nothing else.

If you play cards, then you have rules: a certain card is the king, another card is the queen. You know this is foolishness—no card is the king, and no card is the queen—but if you want to play the game, then certain rules have to be followed. They are rules of the game—nothing is ultimate about them.

You have to follow the traffic rules. Remember: the whole of morality is nothing but traffic rules. You live in a society; you are not alone there, there are many others. Certain rules have to be followed, but they are not ultimate, they have nothing of ultimacy in them. They are just like walking on the left. In America you walk on the right—no problem. If the rule is followed, keep to the right, it is okay. If the rule is followed, keep to the left, it is also okay. Both are the same, but one has to be followed. If you have both rules, then there will be a traffic jam and there will be difficulty, unnecessary difficulty.

When you live with others, the whole of life has to follow certain rules. Those rules are neither religious nor moral nor divine; they are just man-made. One has to be aware, one has to know their relativity; they are formal.

You need not break all the rules; there is no need because then you will be in unnecessary trouble, and rather than becoming a seeker you will become a criminal. Remember that. A seeker is not a soldier, a seeker is not a criminal; a seeker knows that rules are just a game. He is not against them; he transcends them, he goes beyond them. He keeps himself free of them. He follows them for others, but he doesn't become an automaton. He remains conscious, fully alert.

Consciousness is the goal. That is why Chuang Tzu says: "Hence the wise men of old did not lay down one measure for all." They have not laid down any measures, really. They have insisted upon awakening you, through many ways and means. You are so fast asleep, I can hear your snoring! How to awaken you? How to shock you toward awareness? When you are awake, no rules are needed. Still you follow rules—and you know no rules are needed. You don't become a criminal, you transcend and become a seeker.

Get Rid of the Crowd

There is a Sufi story.

A young seeker came to a great Sufi master. As he entered his room and saluted the master with great respect, the master said, "Good. That's perfectly good. What do you want?"

He said, "I want to be initiated."

The master said, "I can initiate you, but what about the crowd that is following you?"

The young man looked back; there was nobody. He said, "What crowd? I am alone."

The master said, "You are not. Just close your eyes and see the crowd."

The young man closed his eyes, and he was surprised. There was the whole crowd that he had left behind: his mother weeping, his father telling him not to go, his wife in tears, his friends preventing him—every face, the whole crowd. And the master said, "Now open your eyes. Can you say that people are not following you?"

He said, "I am sorry. You are right. The whole crowd I am carrying within myself."

So the master said, "Your first work is to get rid of the crowd. This is your problem. And once you are finished with the crowd, things are very simple. The day you are finished with the crowd I will initiate you, because I can only initiate you; I cannot initiate this crowd."

The story is meaningful. Even when you are alone, you are not alone. And a man of meditation, even though in the crowd of thousands of people, is alone.

When you are alone, nobody can see the crowd, because it is within you. And when a meditative man is in the crowd and yet alone, nobody can see his aloneness, because that too is within him.

To know your aloneness is to be acquainted with existence, nature, your reality. And it gives such blissfulness that there is no comparison with any joy that you have felt in the past.

> Unless you can be blissful in your total aloneness, remember, anything that you think is happiness is only a deception.

Many people say that only when they are with others are they perfectly happy. It is not happiness, it is a hallucination of happiness, because your mind is in tune with the people. Alone, they are also in the same trouble as you are. So together there is a certain harmony in the mind, and that harmony gives you the sense of happiness. But the sense is very superficial; it has no roots.

Unless you can be blissful in your total aloneness, remember, anything that you think is happiness is only a deception. And once the thing is clear, it is not difficult to do it. Find time—even for a few minutes, once in a while—just to be alone.

In the beginning you will be miserable, because nobody is there to say how beautiful you are. Nobody is there to say, "What a great artist you are!" There is nobody, just silence around you. But a little patience, and a little alertness not to get identified with the mind, will bring a great revolution.

Happiness and Drugs

One of the most intelligent men of the twentieth century, Aldous Huxley, was very much impressed when LSD was discovered—he was the first promoter of LSD. He lived under the illusion that through LSD you can achieve the same spiritual experiences that Gautam Buddha had, that Kabir had, that Nanak had. Thinking of the *soma* of the Vedas, he wrote in his book, *Heaven and Hell*, that in the future the ultimate drug will be created by science, synthetic. It would be named in honor of the first drug used by the religious people, *soma*. But now there are thousands of people, men and women, suffering in jails for taking drugs.

I see it as the beginning of a search for something beyond the ordinary world, although they are searching in a wrong way. Drugs won't give them reality; they can create a reality, but it is going to last for a few hours, and then they have to take the drug again. And each time they have to take greater and greater quantities because they go on becoming immune.

There has been a great upsurge in demand for drugs which has never been seen before. People are ready to suffer imprisonment, and they come out and they still take drugs. In fact, if they have money they even manage to get drugs from the officers of the jail, the staff of the jail. You just have to give them money.

But I don't see these drugs as a criminal thing; I simply see it as a misdirected younger generation. The intention is right, but there is nobody to tell them that drugs won't fulfill their desire and their longing. Only meditation, only silence, only transcending beyond your mind is going to give you contentment and fulfillment. And they cannot be condemned as they are being condemned and punished. The older generation is responsible because they don't have alternatives for them.

I propose the only alternative: as you become more and more meditative, you don't need anything else. You don't need to create an alternative reality, because you start seeing reality itself. A created reality is just false, it is a dream—maybe a sweet dream, but a dream is a dream, after all.

Their thirst is right. It is just that they are wandering, and their religious leaders, their political leaders, their governments, their educational institutions are not capable of giving them a right direction. I take it as a symptom of a great search that has to be welcomed. Just a right direction has to be given—which the old religions cannot give, which the old society is impotent to give. We need, urgently, the birth of a new human being; we need, urgently, the rebel to change all this sickness and ugliness that is destroying many, many people in the world.

Everybody needs to know himself, his reality. It is good that the desire has arisen. Sooner or later, we will be able to turn people in the right direction. Many people who have become meditators have gone through all the drug trips—and as they became meditators and started meditating, by and by their drugs have disappeared. Now they don't need it. No punishment, no jail, just a right direction—and the reality is so fulfilling, is such a benediction that you cannot expect more.

Existence gives you—in such abundance—richness of being, of love, of peace, of truth, that you cannot ask for more. You cannot even imagine more.

Self-Forgetfulness and Self-Remembrance

These are the two paths: self-forgetfulness, the way of the world, and self-remembrance, the way of godliness. The paradox is that one who seeks happiness never finds it; one who seeks truth and doesn't bother about happiness has always found it.

> The paradox is that one who seeks happiness never finds it.

When you feel one with the truth, everything fits together, falls together. You feel a rhythm, and that rhythm is happiness. You cannot seek it directly. Truth has to be sought. Happiness is found when truth is found, but happiness is not the goal. If you seek happiness directly, you will be more and more unhappy. At the most, your happiness will be just an intoxicant so that you can forget unhappiness; that's all that is going to happen. Happiness is just like a drug—it is LSD, marijuana, mescaline.

Why have so many people in the West come to use drugs? It is a very rational process. It has to come to it because searching for happiness one has to find LSD, sooner or later. The same has happened before in India. In the Vedas they found *soma* because they were seeking happiness; they were not really seekers of truth. They were seeking more and more gratification, and they came to *soma*. *Soma* is the ultimate drug. Whenever a society, an individual, a civilization seeks happiness, somewhere it has to come to drugs, because ultimately, happiness is a search for drugs. The search for happiness is a search to forget oneself; that's what a drug helps you to do. You forget yourself, and there is no misery. You are not there, how can there be misery? You are fast asleep.

> Happiness is found when truth is found, but happiness is not the goal.

The search for truth is just the opposite dimension: not gratification, pleasure, happiness, but asking, "What is the nature of existence? What is true?" One who seeks happiness will never find it—at the most you will find forgetfulness. One who seeks truth will find it, because to seek truth one will have to become true oneself. To seek truth in existence, first you will have to seek the true in your own being. You will become more and more self-remembering.

A Drug Can Only Magnify Your Mood

Drugs can make you happy; they can also make you unhappy, because no drug is guaranteed to give you happiness. The drug can only magnify your mood. If you are unhappy, you will be more unhappy with the drug; you will have nightmares. If you are happy, you will be more happy, madly happy. But you can immediately detect a person who is happy under a drug, for the simple reason that his happiness will be tense. It is just forced on him by chemicals. His face will be smiling but as if somebody is putting a gun behind him and ordering him, "Smile, otherwise I am going to fire."

Chemicals can force you, but the forced smile, the forced happiness will show the tension. And it can only last for hours, then you will fall back into a ditch—deeper than you were before because all that tension has tired your whole system. All that happiness, which was false and forced and chemical, has taken even the little bit of natural happiness that was within you. And once it is gone, you will fall into a deep darkness. And with drugs you will develop a tolerance, so soon you will need more quantity, then more quantity, then more quantity, and a moment comes . . .

The "Drug Problem"

The drug problem is nothing new; it is as ancient as mankind. There has never been a time when man was not in search of escape. The most ancient book in the world is the Rigveda, and it is full of drug use. The name of the drug is *soma*. Since those ancient times, all the religions have tried to get people not to use drugs. All the governments have been against drugs. Yet drugs have proved more powerful than governments or religions because nobody has looked into the very psychology of the drug user.

People are miserable. They live in anxiety, anguish, and frustration. There seems to be no way out except drugs. The only way to prevent the use of drugs will be to make people joyful, happy, blissful.

I am also against drugs for the simple reason that they help you to forget your misery for a time. They do not prepare you to fight misery and suffering; rather they weaken you. But the reasons that religions and governments are against drugs and my reasons for being against drugs are totally different. They want people to remain miserable and frustrated, because the person in suffering is never rebellious; he is tortured in his own being, he is falling apart. He cannot conceive of a better society, of a better culture, of a better human being. Because of his misery he becomes an easy victim of the priests because they console him, because they say to him, "Blessed are the poor, blessed are the meek, blessed are those who suffer, because they shall inherit the kingdom of God."

The suffering humanity is also in the hands of the politicians because the suffering humanity needs some hope—hope of a classless society somewhere in the future, hope of a society where there will be no poverty, no hunger, no misery. In short, they can manage and be patient with their sufferings if they have a utopia just close to the horizon. And you must note the meaning of the word *utopia*. It means that which never happens! It is just like the horizon; it is so close that you think you can run and meet the place where earth and sky meet. But you can go on running your whole life and never meet the place because there is no such place. It is a hallucination.

The politician lives on promises; the priest lives on promises. In the last ten thousand years, nobody has delivered the goods.

> In the last ten thousand years, nobody has delivered the goods.

Their reason for being against drugs is that drugs destroy their whole business. If people start taking opium, hashish, LSD, they don't care about communism, and they don't care about what is going to happen tomorrow, they don't care about life after death, they don't care about God or paradise. They are fulfilled in the moment.

So my reasons are different. I am also against drugs, not because they cut the roots of the religions and the politicians, but because they destroy your inner growth toward spirituality. They prevent you from reaching the Promised Land. You remain hanging around the hallucinations while you are capable of reaching the real. Drugs give you a toy.

But since drugs are not going to disappear, I would like every government, every scientific lab, to purify drugs, to make them healthier without any side effects, which is possible now. We can create a drug like the one which Aldous Huxley, in memory of the

Rigveda, called *soma*, which will be without any bad effects—which will not be addictive, which will be a joy, a happiness, a dance, a song.

If we cannot make it possible for everybody to become a Gautam Buddha, we have no right to prevent people from at least having illusory glimpses of the aesthetic state, which Gautam Buddha must have known. Perhaps these small experiences will lead the person to explore more. Sooner or later that person is going to be fed up with the drug because it will go on repeating the same scene again and again. Howsoever beautiful a scene is, repetition makes it a boredom.

So first, purify the drug from all bad effects. Second, let people who want to enjoy, enjoy. They will become bored by it. And then their only path will be to seek some method of meditation to find the ultimate bliss.

The question is basically concerned with the younger generation of people. The generation gap is the world's very latest phenomenon; it never used to exist. In the past, children of six and seven started using their hands, their minds, with their families in their traditional professions. By the time they were fourteen they were already craftsmen, workers; they were married, they had responsibilities. By the time they were twenty or twenty-four they had their own children, so there was never a gap between the generations. Each generation overlapped the other generation. Now, for the first time in the history of humanity the generation gap has happened. It is of tremendous importance. Now, for the first time, up to the age of twenty-five or twenty-six, when you come back from the university, you have no responsibility, no children, no worries, and you have the whole world before you to dream about—how to better it, how to make it richer, how to create a race of superhumans. These are the years, between fourteen and twenty-four, when one is a dreamer, when the whole of one's energy is available to dream. You can become a communist, a socialist, all sorts of things. And this is the time when one starts feeling frustrated, because the way the world works—the bureaucracy, the government, the politicians, the society, the religion—it does not seem that you will be able to create a reality out of your dreams.

You come home from the university full of ideas, and every idea is going to be crushed by the society. Soon you forget about the new humanity and the new age. You cannot even find employment; you cannot feed yourself. How can you think of a classless society where there will be no rich and no poor?

It is this moment when people turn toward drugs; they give a temporary relief. But most drugs, as they are right now, are addictive, so you have to go on increasing the dose. And they are destructive to the body, to the brain; soon you are absolutely helpless. You cannot live without drugs, and with drugs there is no space in life for you.

But I don't say that the younger generation are responsible for it—and to punish them and put them in jail is sheer stupidity. They are not criminals, they are victims.

My idea is that education should be divided into two parts: one intellectual and the other practical. From the very beginning, a child enters school not just to learn the three R's, but also to learn to create something—some craftsmanship, some skill. Half of the time should be given to intellectual pursuits, and half of the time should be given to life's real necessities; that will keep the balance. And by the time he comes out of the university, he will not be a utopian, and he will not be in need of employment by others. He will be able to create things on his own.

And for students who feel any kind of frustration, from the very beginning things should be changed. If they are frustrated, perhaps they are not studying the right stuff. Perhaps they want to become a carpenter, and you are making them a doctor; they want to become a gardener, and you are making them an engineer. Great psychological understanding will be needed so that each child is sent in the direction where they will learn something. And in every school, every college, every university, at least one hour of meditation for everybody must be compulsory so that whenever one feels frustrated or depressed, one has a space within himself that he can move to and immediately can get rid of all the depression and frustration. He need not turn to drugs. Meditation is the answer.

> And in every school, every college, every university, at least one hour of meditation for everybody must be compulsory.

But rather than doing all these things, the people who are in power go on doing idiotic things—prohibition, punishment. They know that for ten thousand years we have been prohibiting, and we have not succeeded. If you prohibit alcohol, more people become alcoholic, and a more dangerous kind of alcohol becomes available. Thousands of people die by poisoning, and who is responsible?

Now they are punishing people for years in jail without even understanding that if a person has taken a drug or has been addicted to a drug, he needs treatment, not punishment. He should be sent to a place where he can be taken care of, where he can be taught meditation, and slowly, slowly, can be directed from the drugs toward something better.

Instead they are forcing people into jails—ten years in jail. They don't value human life at all! If you give ten years in jail to a young man of twenty, you have wasted his most precious time— and without any benefit, because in jail every drug is more easily available than anywhere else. The inmates are all highly skilled drug users, who become teachers for those who are amateurs. After ten years the person will come out perfectly trained. One thing only your jails teach: anything you do is not wrong unless you are caught; just don't be caught. And there are masters who can teach you how not to be caught again.

So this whole thing is absolutely absurd. I am also against drugs but in a totally different way.

Choicelessness Is Bliss

The first thing to be understood is that life is very para-doxical, and because of that many things happen. These are the two alternatives: either man can be in heaven or hell. And there is no third possibility. Either you can be in deep suffering, or you can be without suffering and in deep bliss. These are the only two possibilities, two openings, two doors, two modes of being.

Then the question necessarily arises why man chooses to be in suffering. Man never chooses to be in suffering, man always chooses to be in bliss—and there comes the paradox. If you choose to be in bliss, you will be in suffering, because to be in bliss means to be choiceless. This is the problem. If you choose to be in bliss, you will be in suffering. If you don't choose, if you simply remain a witness, non-choosing, you will be in bliss. So it is not a question of choosing between bliss and suffering; deep down it is a question of choosing between choosing and non-choosing.

Why does it happen that whenever you choose you are in suffering?—because choice divides life: something has to be cut and thrown away. You don't accept the total. You accept something in it and you deny something, that's what choice means. And life is a totality. If you choose something and deny something, that which you deny will come to you because life cannot be divided. And that which you deny, just because you deny it, becomes a powerful thing over you. You really become afraid of it.

Nothing can be denied. You can only close your eyes to it. You can only escape. You can become inattentive toward it, but it is always there hidden, waiting for the moment to assert. So if you deny suffering—if you say you are not going to choose suffering—then in a subtle way you have chosen it. Now it will always be around you. One thing.

> So when you cling to happiness, you are again creating suffering, because this happiness will pass away.

Life is totality—the first thing; and life is change—the second thing. These are basic truths. You cannot divide life. Secondly: nothing is stagnant and nothing can be. So when you say, "I am not going to suffer. I am going to choose a blissful mode of living," you will cling to happiness. And whenever you cling to something, you want it, you hope it to be permanent. And nothing can be permanent in life. Life is a flux.

So when you cling to happiness, you are again creating suffering, because this happiness will pass away; nothing can remain. It is a river, and the moment you cling to a river, you are creating a situation in which you will be frustrated, because the river will move. Sooner or later you will find that the river has gone far away. It is not now with you: your hands are empty and your heart is frustrated.

If you cling to bliss, there will be moments of bliss, but they are going to pass away. Life is a flux. Nothing can be permanent here except you. Except you, nothing is eternal here, and if you cling to a changing thing, when it is gone you will suffer. And it is not only that when it is gone you will suffer; if you have the mind of clinging, while it is there you will not be able to enjoy it, because you will be constantly afraid that it is going to be lost.

If you cling you will miss the opportunity also. Later on you will suffer and right now you will not enjoy, because the fear is just around the corner—sooner or later it has to go. The guest has come to your house, and you know he is a guest and tomorrow morning he will leave. You start suffering for the future—tomorrow morning he will leave—and that pain, that suffering, that anguish, comes upon you right now. You cannot be happy while the guest is in your home. While the guest is with you, you cannot be happy, because you are already in anxiety and anguish that tomorrow morning he will leave. So while he is there you will not be happy, and when he is gone you will be unhappy. This is what is happening.

Life Is a Rhythm of Opposites

The first thing: life cannot be divided. If you divide, only then can you choose. And that which you choose is flux-like—sooner or later it will be gone—and that which you have denied will fall over you; you cannot escape it. You cannot say, "I will live only in the days, and I will escape the nights." You cannot say, "I will live only with the ingoing breath, and I will not allow the outgoing breaths."

Life is a rhythm of opposites. The breath comes in and goes out: between these two opposites—ingoing and outgoing—you exist. Suffering is there; happiness is there. Happiness is just like the ingoing breath; suffering is just like the outgoing breath or day and night—the rhythm of opposites. You cannot say, "I will live only if I am happy. When I am not happy, I will not live." You can take this attitude, but this attitude will make you suffer more.

No one chooses suffering, remember. You ask why man has chosen to suffer. No one has chosen to suffer. You have chosen not to suffer, you have chosen to be happy, and you have chosen strongly. You are doing everything to be happy, and that's why you are in suffering, why you are not happy.

So what is to be done? Remember that life is total. You cannot choose—the whole life has to be lived. There will be moments of happiness and there will be moments of suffering, and both have to be lived; you cannot choose. Because life is both—otherwise the rhythm will be lost, and without rhythm there will be no life.

It is just like music. You hear some music: there are notes, sounds, and after each sound there is silence, a gap. Because of that gap, that interval of silence, and the sound—because of both the opposites—music is created. If you say, "I will choose only sounds, and I am not going to take the gaps," there will be no music. It will be a monotonous thing; it will be dead. Those gaps give life to sound. This is the beauty of life—that through opposites it exists. Sound and silence, sound and silence—that creates music, the rhythm. The same is with life. Suffering and happiness are two opposites. You cannot choose.

If you choose, you have become a victim; you will suffer. If you become aware of this totality of the opposites and the way that life functions, you don't choose—the first thing. And when you don't choose, there is no need to cling, there is no meaning in clinging. When suffering comes, you enjoy the suffering, and when happiness comes, you enjoy the happiness. When the guest is at home, you enjoy him; when he has gone, you enjoy the suffering, the absence, the pain. I say enjoy both. This is the path of wisdom: enjoy both—don't choose. Whatsoever falls upon you, accept it. It is your fate, it is how life is, and nothing can be done about it.

> Suffering and happiness are two opposites. You cannot choose.

If you take this attitude, there is no choosing. You have become choiceless. And when you are choiceless, you will become aware of yourself because now you are not worried about what happens, so you are not outgoing. You are not worried about what is happening around you. Whatsoever happens you will enjoy it, you will live it, you will go through it, you will experience it, and you will gain something out of it, because every experience is an expansion of consciousness.

If there is really no suffering, you will be poor for it because suffering gives you depth. A man who has not suffered will always remain on the surface. Suffering gives you depth. Really, if there is no suffering, you will be saltless. You will be nothing, just a boring phenomenon. Suffering gives you tone, a keenness. A quality comes to you which only suffering can give, which no happiness can give. A man who has remained always in happiness, in comfort, who has not suffered, will not have any tone. He will be just a lump of being. There cannot be any depth. Really, there cannot be any heart. The heart is created through suffering; through pain you evolve.

If a man has only suffered and he has not known any happiness, then too he will not be rich, because richness comes through opposites. The more you move in opposites, the higher, the deeper you evolve. A man who has simply suffered will become a slave. He who has not known any moments of happiness will not be really alive. He will become an animal; he will just exist anyhow. There will be no poetry, no song in the heart, no hope in the eyes. He will settle down to his pessimistic existence. There will be no struggle, no adventure. He will not move. He will be simply a stagnant pool of consciousness, and a stagnant pool of consciousness is not conscious—by and by he will become unconscious. That's why if there is too much pain, you fall unconscious.

So just happiness will not be of much help, because there will be no challenge. Just pain will not be of much growth, because there will be nothing to struggle, to hope, to dream; there will be no fantasy. Both are needed, and life exists between both as a very delicate tension, a subtle tension.

If you understand this, then you don't choose. Then you know how life functions, how life is. This is the way, this is the way of life—it moves through happiness, it moves through suffering and gives you tone and gives you meaning and gives you depth. So both are good.

I say both are good. I don't say choose between the two—I say both are good, don't choose. Rather, enjoy both; rather, allow both to happen. Be open without any resistance. Don't cling to one, and don't resist the other.

Let no-resistance be your motto: I will not resist life. Whatsoever life gives to me, I will be ready to take it, available, and I will enjoy it. The nights are also good and beautiful, and suffering has a beauty of its own. No happiness can have that beauty. Darkness has its own beauty; day has its own beauty. There is no comparison, and there is no choice. Both have their own dimensions to work in.

The moment this consciousness arises in you, you will not choose. You will be just a witness, and you will enjoy—this choicelessness will become bliss. Bliss is not contrary to suffering; bliss is a quality which you can bring to anything whatsoever—even to suffering.

A Buddha cannot suffer, but that doesn't mean that suffering doesn't happen to him. Remember, suffering happens as much to Buddha as it happens to you, but he cannot suffer because he knows the art of enjoying it. He cannot suffer because he remains blissful. Even in suffering he remains festive, meditative, alive, enjoying, open, non-resistant. Suffering happens to him, but he is not touched. Suffering comes and goes, just like a breath coming in and going out. He remains himself. The suffering cannot push him aside. The suffering cannot push him off his feet. Nothing can push him—neither suffering nor happiness. You exist like a pendulum: everything pushes you—everything. You cannot even be really happy, because happiness will also kill you. You get so involved in it.

I remember, once it happened that a poor schoolmaster— very old, poor, retired—won a lottery. The wife was afraid, and she thought, "This is going to be too much for the old man. Five thousand dollars is too much for him. Even a five dollar note gives him so much happiness, so five thousand dollars may kill him."

She ran to the church, to the nearby church, and went to the priest and told him what had happened. She said, "The old man is out, but he is just coming back, this is his time to return, so do something. Five thousand dollars—just the news will kill him!"

The priest said, "Don't be afraid. I know the human mind and the way it functions. I know the psychology. I will come." So the priest came to the house. The moment they arrived the old man also arrived, so the priest started. He said, "Suppose you won a lottery of five thousand dollars—what would you do?"

The old man thought about it, pondered over it, and he said, "I would give half of the money to the church."

The priest fell down dead. It was too much.

Even happiness will kill you because you get so involved. You cannot remain out of anything. Suffering or happiness, whatsoever comes to your door, you get so involved in it you are just pushed off your feet. You are no more there. Just a breeze comes in the house and you are no more there.

What I am saying is that if you don't choose, if you remain alert and aware that this is how life is—days and nights come and go, suffering and happiness—you just witness. There is no clinging to happiness, no hankering for happiness, and no escape from suffering. You remain in yourself—centered, rooted. This is what bliss is.

So remember, bliss is not something opposite to suffering. Don't think that when you become blissful there will be no suffering—nonsense. Suffering is part of life. It ceases only when you are not. When you completely disappear from the body, suffering ceases. When there is no birth, suffering ceases. But then you are lost in the totality, then you are no more—just a drop has fallen into the ocean and is no more.

While you are, suffering will continue. It is part of life. But you can become aware: then suffering happens somewhere around you, but it never happens to you. But then happiness also never happens to you. Don't think that happiness will go on happening to you and suffering will not happen—both will not happen to you. They will just happen around, just on the periphery, and you will be centered in yourself. You will see them happening, you will enjoy them happening, but they will happen around you; they will not happen to you.

This becomes possible if you don't choose. That's why I said this is delicate, subtle. Because of the paradoxical life, you choose happiness and you fall in suffering. You try to escape from suffering, and more and more suffering is invited. So you can take it as an ultimate law: whatsoever you choose, the opposite will be your fate. Say it as an ultimate law: whatsoever you choose, the opposite will be your fate.

Witnessing Is You

So whatsoever is your fate, remember, you have chosen it by choosing the opposite. If you are suffering, you have chosen your suffering by choosing happiness. Don't choose happiness, and suffering disappears. Don't choose at all. Then nothing can happen to you, and everything is a flux except you. That has to be understood very deeply.

Only you are the constant factor in existence, nothing else. Only you are the eternity, nothing else. Your awareness is never

> Don't choose happiness, and suffering disappears. Don't choose at all.

a flux. Suffering comes; you witness it. Then happiness comes; you witness it. Then nothing comes; you witness it. Only one thing remains constant—witnessing—and witnessing is you.

You were a child . . . Or, if you move even further backward, once you were just an atomic cell. You cannot even imagine it—just an atomic cell in your mother's womb, not even visible to the naked eyes. If that cell comes before you, and you encounter it, you will not be able to recognize that once you were that. Then you were a child, then you became young, and now you are old or lying on your deathbed. Many things happened. Your whole life has been a flux; nothing remained the same for even two moments.

Heraclitus says you cannot step twice in the same river—and this he says for the river of life. You cannot have two similar moments. The moment that has gone cannot be repeated. It is gone forever; you cannot have it again. The same cannot exist. In such a great flux, only one thing within you remains the same—the witnessing.

If you could have witnessed in your mother's womb, the quality of consciousness would have been the same. If you could have witnessed when you were a child, the quality of witnessing would have been the same. Young or dying, while just dying on your bed, if you can witness, the quality of consciousness will be the same.

The only one thing deep down within you is your witnessing self, your consciousness—that remains the same; everything else changes. And if you cling to any object of the world of change, you will suffer. Nothing can be done about it. You are trying to do the impossible, that's why you suffer. I know you never choose, but that is not the point. If you suffer, you have chosen it indirectly.

Once you become aware of this indirectness of life, this paradoxical quality of life, you will stop choosing. When choice falls, the world has disappeared. When choosing falls, you have entered the absolute.

But that is possible only when the choosing mind disappears

completely. A choiceless awareness is needed, and then you will be in bliss. Rather, you will be the bliss. And I will repeat again: suffering will continue to happen, but now nothing can make you suffer. Even if you are suddenly thrown into hell, just by your presence there, for you it will be a hell no more.

Someone asked Socrates where he would like to go, so Socrates said, "I don't know whether there is a hell and a heaven. I don't know whether they are there or not, but I will not choose between them. My only prayer will be this: allow me to be alert wherever I am. Let me be fully aware wherever I am. Whether it is hell or heaven, that is irrelevant." Because if you

> You carry your hell and heaven within you.

are fully alert, hell disappears—hell is your being not aware. If you are fully aware, heaven appears—heaven is your being fully aware.

Really there are no such geographical places as hell or heaven. And don't go on thinking in childish terms that someday you will die, and God will send you to heaven or hell according to your doings, according to whatsoever you have done on earth. No, you carry your hell and heaven within you. Wherever you move, you carry your hell or heaven with you.

Even God cannot do anything. If suddenly you meet him, he will look like a hell. You carry your hell within you; you project it wherever you are. You will suffer. The encounter will be just death-like, intolerable. You may become unconscious. Whatsoever happens

> It is your choice
> and you are
> responsible.
> No one else is
> responsible.

to you, you carry within you. The seed of consciousness is the seed of the whole existence.

So remember, if you suffer, you have chosen it: consciously, unconsciously, directly, indirectly, you have chosen it. It is your choice and you are responsible. No one else is responsible.

But in our mind, in our confused mind, everything is upside-down. If you suffer, you think you suffer because of others. You suffer because of you. No one can make you suffer. That is impossible. And even if someone makes you suffer, it is your choice to be in suffering through him. You have chosen him and you have chosen a particular type of suffering through him. No one can make you suffer—it is your choice. But you always go on thinking that if the other changes, or if the other is doing something else, you will not suffer.

I have heard. Mulla Nasruddin was filling out a report because he had crashed his car into a parked car. He was filling out a report, and many things were asked. When he came to the part where it was asked what the driver of the other vehicle could have done to avoid the accident, he filled it, "The car was parked there; he should have parked it somewhere else— because of him, the accident has happened."

And this is what you are doing. Always the other is responsible: he should have done something or other, and there would have been no suffering. No, the other is not responsible at all. You are responsible, and unless you take this responsibility consciously upon you, you will not change. The change will become possible, easily possible, the moment you realize that you are responsible for it.

If you have suffered, it was your choice. This is what the law of karma is, nothing else: you are wholly responsible. Whatsoever happens—suffering or happiness, hell or heaven—whatsoever happens, ultimately you are totally responsible. This is what the law of karma is: total responsibility is with you.

But don't be afraid, don't be scared by it, because if the total responsibility is with you, then suddenly a door of freedom opens—because if you are the cause of your suffering, you can change. If others are the cause, then you cannot change. Then how can you change? Unless the whole world changes, you will suffer. And there seems to be no way to change others—then suffering cannot end.

But we are so pessimistic that even such beautiful doctrines as the law of karma we interpret in such a way that they don't free and liberate us, but rather, on the contrary, they make us more burdened. In India the law of karma has been known for at least five thousand years or even more, but what have we done? It is not that we have taken responsibility upon ourselves; we have thrown all the responsibility on the law of karma—that it is happening because of the law of karma and we cannot do anything, nothing can be done; because of the past lives this life is such.

The law of karma was to free you. It was giving you total

freedom toward yourself. No one else can make any suffering for you—this was the message. If you are suffering, you have created it. You are the master of your fate, and if you want to change it, immediately you can change it, and the life will be different. But the attitude . . .

I have heard, once two friends were talking. One was a bona fide optimist, the other a bona fide pessimist. Even the optimist was not too happy about the situation. The optimist said, "If this economic crisis continues and these political catastrophes continue and the world remains the same as it is, immoral, then we are going to be reduced to begging soon."

Even he was not too hopeful about it—the optimist. When he said, "We are going to be reduced to begging," the pessimist said, "From whom? From whom are you going to beg if this condition continues?"

You have a mind, and you go on bringing your mind to everything. Really, you transform the quality of every teaching and doctrine. You defeat Buddhas and Krishnas so easily because you convert the whole thing; you color it in your own way.

You are totally responsible for whatsoever you are and for whatsoever world you are living in. It is your creation. If this goes deep in you, you can change everything. You need not suffer. Don't choose, be a witness, and bliss will happen to you. Bliss is not a dead state. Suffering will go on continuing around you. So it is not a question of what happens to you; it is a question of how you are. The total, ultimate meaning comes from you, not from the happening.

Thy Will Be Done

One day a man came, a farmer, an old farmer, and he said, "Look, you may be God, and you may have created the world, but one thing I must say to you: you are not a farmer, and you don't know even the abc of farming. And your whole nature and the functioning of your nature is so absurd, and this I say out of my whole life's experience. You have to learn something."

God said, "What's your advice?"

The farmer said, "You give me one year's time and just let things be according to me and see what happens. There will be no poverty left!"

God was willing, and one year was given to the farmer. Now it was according to his will that everything was happening. Naturally, he asked the best, he thought only of the best—no thunder, no strong winds, no dangers for the crop. Everything comfortable, cozy, and he was very happy. The wheat was growing so high! No dangers were there, no hindrances were there; everything was moving according to his desire. When he wanted sun, there was sun; when he wanted rain, there was rain, and as much as he wanted. In the old days, sometimes it rained too much, and the rivers would be flooded and the crops would be destroyed, and sometimes it would not rain enough, and the land would remain dry and the crops would die . . . and sometimes something else, and sometimes something else. It was rare, very rare, that things were right. But this year everything was put right, mathematically right.

The wheat was growing so high that the farmer was very happy. He used to go to God and say, "Look! This time the crops will be such that for ten years if people don't work, there will be enough food."

But when the crops were cut, there was no wheat inside. He was surprised—what happened?! He asked God, "What happened? What went wrong?"

God said, "Because there was no challenge, because there was no difficulty, because there was no conflict, no friction, because all was good, you avoided all that was bad, the wheat remained impotent. A little struggle is a must. Storms are needed, thunder, lightning is needed. They shake up the soul inside the wheat."

This parable is of immense value. If you are just happy and happy and happy, happiness will lose all meaning. You will become tired of it. You will be fed up with it. You remain interested in happiness because there are sad moments too. Those sad moments keep you interested in happiness. You cannot go on eating only sugar and sugar and sugar—something salted is a must, otherwise all taste will be lost.

If you are just happy, just happy, just happy . . . you will have diabetes from happiness. You will become impotent. You will be bored, utterly bored—your life will not have meaning. It will be as if somebody is writing with white chalk on a white wall. He can go on writing, but nobody will ever be able to read it. You have to write on a blackboard; then it comes clear and loud. The night is as much needed as the day. And the days of sadness are as essential as the days of happiness.

This I call understanding. Once you understand it, you re-

lax—in that relaxation is surrender. You say: "Thy will be done."
You say: "Do whatsoever you feel is right. If today clouds are
needed, give me clouds. Don't listen to me. My understanding
is tiny. My will is foolish. What do I know of life and its secrets?
Don't listen to me! You just go on doing your will."

And, slowly, slowly the more you see the rhythm of life, the
rhythm of duality, the rhythm of polarity; you stop asking, you
stop choosing. Not that by choosing anything changes—nothing
changes, just you become frustrated. Everything remains the
same. If the river is going north, the river is going north; by your
choosing that the river should go south, you become miserable,
that's all. The river continues to go north!

Your will, your choice, your action, makes no difference at all.
But one difference, certainly, it makes—no difference in the situation
of the world, in existence—but
one difference in your psychology: you become frustrated, because the river is not going north,
or going north, and you have
the opposite direction in your
mind. You are failing. Not that
the river intends to make you a
failure—the river has nothing
to do with you. The river is simply going north.

> The man of
> understanding goes
> with the river, flows
> with the flow, moves
> with the wind.

The man of understanding goes with the river, flows with the
flow, moves with the wind. Slowly, slowly the understanding that
"Nothing is in my hands" becomes surrender. And that surrender
brings great benediction. That surrender brings bliss.

You have found the secret! This is the secret. Live with this secret, and see the beauty. Live with this secret, and you will be suddenly surprised: How great is the blessing of life! How much is being showered on you every moment! But you are living in your expectations, in your small, tiny, trivial desires. And because things are not fitting with your desires, you are miserable.

Misery has only one meaning: that things are not fitting with your desires—and things never fit with your desires, they cannot. Things simply go on following their nature.

Lao Tzu calls this nature Tao. Buddha calls this nature Dhamma. Mahavira has defined religion as the nature of things. Nothing can be done. Fire is hot and water is cool. Don't try to impose your will on the nature of things. That is what the stupid man goes on doing—and creates misery for himself, creates hell. The wise man is one who relaxes with the nature of things, who follows the nature of things.

And when you follow the nature of things, no shadow is cast. There is no misery. Even sadness is luminous then, even sadness has a beauty then. Not that sadness will not come—it will come—but it will not be your enemy. You will befriend it because you will see its necessity. You will be able to see its grace, and you will be able to see why it is there and why it is needed. And without it, you will be less, not more.

Beyond Sadness

When sadness comes, accept it. Listen to its song. It has something to give to you. It has a gift that no happiness can give to you. Only sadness can give it.

Happiness is always shallow—sadness, always deep. Happiness is like a wave; sadness is like the innermost depth of an ocean. In sad-

> When sadness comes, accept it. Listen to its song.

ness you remain with yourself, left alone. In happiness you start moving with people, you start sharing. In sadness you close your eyes, you delve deep within yourself. Sadness has a song—a very deep phenomenon is sadness. Accept it. Enjoy it. Taste it without any rejection, and you will see that it brings many gifts to you that no happiness can ever bring.

If you can accept sadness, it is no longer sadness. You have brought a new quality to it. You will grow through it. Now it will not be a stone, a rock on the path blocking the way; it will become a step.

And remember always: a person who has not known deep sadness is a poor person. He will never have an inner richness. A person who has lived always happy, smiling, shallow, has not entered the innermost temple of his being. He has missed the innermost shrine.

Remain capable of moving with all the polarities. When sadness comes, be really sad. Don't try to escape from it; allow it, cooperate with it, let it dissolve in you and you be dissolved in it. Become one with it. Be really sad—no resistance, no conflict, no struggle. When happiness comes, be happy, dance, be ecstatic. When happiness comes, don't try to cling to it. Don't say it should remain always and always. That is the way to miss it. When sadness comes, don't say, "Don't come to me," or, "If you have come, please go soon." That is the way to miss it.

Don't reject sadness and don't cling to happiness, and soon you will understand that happiness and sadness are two aspects of the same coin. And then you will see that happiness also has a sadness in it, and sadness also has a happiness in it. Then your inner being is enriched. Then you can enjoy everything—the morning and the evening also, the sunlight and the dark night also, the day and the night, the summer and the winter, life and death. You can enjoy all.

When you don't have a choice, you are already transcendental. You have transcended. Then the duality doesn't divide you. You remain undivided, and this is advait, this is what Shankara means when he says "non-dualism." This is what the Upanishads teach—to be non-dual, to be one.

To be one means not to choose, because once you choose, your choice divides you. You say, "I would like to be happy, and I don't want to be unhappy"; you are divided. Simply say, "Whatever happens, everything is welcome. My doors are open. Sadness comes—come be my guest. Happiness comes—come be my guest. I will be a host to everything—with no rejection, with no choice, with no like, no dislike."

Suddenly nobody can divide you. You have attained an inner unity, an inner melody, an inner music, an inner harmony.

Responses to Questions

Somewhere there is a fear which makes me closed and hard and sad and desperate and angry and hopeless. It seems to be so subtle that I don't even get really in touch with it. How can I see it more clearly?

THE ONLY PROBLEM WITH SADNESS, desperateness, anger, hopelessness, anxiety, anguish, misery, is that you want to get rid of them. That's the only barrier.

You will have to live with them. You cannot just escape. They are the very situation in which life has to integrate and grow. They are the challenges of life. Accept them. They are blessings in disguise. If you want to escape from them, if you somehow want to get rid of them, then the problem arises—because if you want to get rid of something, you never look at it directly. And then the thing starts hiding from you because you are condemnatory; then the thing goes on moving deeper into the unconscious, hides in the darkest corner of your being where you cannot find it. It moves into the basement of your being and hides there. And of course the deeper it goes, the more trouble it creates—because then it starts functioning from unknown corners of your being, and you are completely helpless.

So the first thing is: never repress. The first thing is: whatsoever is the case is the case. Accept it and let it come—let it come in front of you. In fact, just to say "do not repress" is not enough. If you allow me, I would like to say, "Befriend it." You are feeling sad? Befriend it, have compassion for it. Sadness also has a being. Allow it, embrace it, sit with it, hold hands with it. Be friendly. Be in love with it. Sadness is beautiful. Nothing is wrong with it. Who told you that something is wrong in being sad? In fact, only sadness gives you depth. Laughter is shallow; happiness is skin-deep. Sadness goes to the very bones, to the marrow. Nothing goes as deep as sadness.

So don't be worried. Remain with it, and sadness will take you to your innermost core. You can ride on it, and you will be able to know a few new things about your being that you had never known before. Those things can be revealed only in a sad state; they can never be revealed in a happy state. Darkness is also good, and darkness is also divine. The day is not only God's; the night is his also. I call this attitude religious.

"Somewhere there is a fear which makes me closed and hard and sad and desperate and angry and hopeless. It seems to be so subtle that I don't even really get in touch with it."

It becomes subtle if you want to get rid of it. Then, of course, it protects itself, it hides in the deepest corners of your being. It becomes so subtle and so garbed that you cannot recognize it. It starts coming under different names. If you are very much against anger, then anger will arise under a different name—it may become pride, it may become ego, it may become even a religious pride, it may become even pious. It may hide behind your virtues; it may start hiding behind your character. Then it becomes very subtle because now the label is changed. It is playing somebody else's role, but deep down it remains anger.

Let things be as they are. This is what courage is: to allow things as they are.

I am not promising you any rose garden—there are thorns. Roses also, but you can reach the roses only when you have passed the thorns. One who has never been sad cannot really be happy. It is impossible to be happy. Your happiness will be just a forced gesture—empty, impotent. You can see it on people's faces when they laugh: their laugh is so shallow, it is just painted on their lips. It has no relationship with their heart; it is absolutely unconnected.

It is just like lipstick—the lips look red and rosy, but that redness does not come from the redness of the blood. It is good if lips are red, but the redness should come from aliveness, from your blood cells, from your energy, vitality, youth. Now, you paint your lips—they look red, but it is ugly. Lipstick is ugly. The whole thing seems to be absurd. If your lips are red, vital, alive, what is the point of painting them? You are making them ugly and false.

Your happiness is also like lipstick. You are not happy, and you know you are not happy, but you cannot accept the fact because that would be too shattering for your ego. You—and not happy?! How can you accept it? Maybe you are not happy inside, but that is your own problem; you must not express it, you are not to say the truth. For the world, you have to keep a face, you have to maintain a personality. So you go on laughing. Watch people's laughter, and you will immediately see which laughter comes from the heart. When laughter comes from the heart, you can immediately feel a different vibe—an overflowing. That person is really happy. When laughter is just on the lips, it is empty. It is just a gesture; nothing is behind it. It is a facade.

The one who cannot laugh deeply is the one who has repressed sadness—he cannot go deep because he is afraid of sadness. Even if he goes deep into his laughter, there is a fear that sadness may surface, may bubble up. He has to be always on guard.

So please, whatsoever the situation is, start allowing it. If you are sad, you are sad. This is what existence means for you—at this moment, at least, it wants you to be sad. So be true—be sad! Live this sadness. And if you can live this sadness, a different quality of happiness will arise in you; it will not be a repression of sadness, it will be beyond sadness.

> A person who can be patiently sad will suddenly find that one morning happiness is arising in the heart from some unknown source.

A person who can be patiently sad will suddenly find that one morning happiness is arising in the heart from some unknown source. That unknown source is existence. You have earned it if you have been truly sad; if you have been truly hopeless, desperate, unhappy, miserable, if you have lived in hell, you have earned heaven. You have paid the cost.

I was reading a joke:

Mr. Goldberg came home from the office unexpectedly and found his wife in bed with Mr. Cohen, the next-door neighbor.

Distraught and angry, he ran next door and confronted Mrs. Cohen.

"Mrs. Cohen!" he cried. "Your husband is in bed with my wife."

"Calm down! Calm down!" Mrs. Cohen said. "Look, don't take it so hard. Sit down, have a cup of tea. Relax."

Mr. Goldberg sat quietly and drank his cup of tea. It was then that he noticed a little glint in Mrs. Cohen's eye.

Coyly she suggested, "You want a little revenge?"

And with that they withdrew to the couch and made love. Then they had another cup of tea, then a little more revenge, a little more tea, more revenge, more tea . . .

Finally Mrs. Cohen looked at Mr. Goldberg and asked, "How about another revenge?"

"I will tell you, Mrs. Cohen," said Mr. Goldberg quietly, "to be truthful, I've got no hard feelings left."

Whatsoever the situation, if you are sad, be sad; if you are in a revengeful mood, take your revenge; if you are jealous, be jealous; if you are angry, be angry. Never avoid the fact. You have to live it; that is part of life's progress, growth, evolution. Those who avoid remain immature. If you want to remain immature then go on avoiding; but remember, you are avoiding life itself. Whatsoever you are avoiding is not the point; the very avoiding is an avoidance of life.

Confront life. Encounter life. Difficult moments will be there, but one day you will see that those difficult moments gave you strength because you encountered them. They were meant to be. Those difficult moments are hard when you are passing through them, but later on you will see they have made you more integrated. Without them you would never have been centered, grounded.

The old religions all over the world have been repressive; the new religion of the future is going to be expressive. And I teach that new religion. Let expression be one of the most fundamental rules of your life. Even if you have to suffer for it, suffer. You will never be a loser. That suffering will make you more and more capable of enjoying life, of rejoicing in life.

How can I be myself?

THAT SHOULD BE THE EASIEST THING in the world, but it is not. To be oneself one need not do anything; one already is. How can you be otherwise? How can you be anybody else? But I can understand the problem. The problem arises because society corrupts everybody. Society up to now has been a great corruption. It corrupts the mind, the being. It enforces things on you and you lose contact with yourself. It tries to make something out of you other than that which you were meant to be. It puts you off your center. It drags you away from yourself. It teaches you to be like a Christ or to be like a Buddha or to be like this and that. It never says to you to be yourself. It never allows you freedom to be. It enforces foreign, outside images on your mind.

Then the problem arises. You can pretend at the most, and when you pretend, you are never satisfied. You always want to be yourself—that is natural, and the society does not allow it. It wants you to be somebody else. It wants you to be phony. It does not want you to be real, because real people are dangerous people; real people are rebellious people. Real people cannot be controlled so easily, real people cannot be regimented. Real people will live their reality in their own way—they will do their thing, they won't bother about other things. You cannot sacrifice them. In the name of religion, in the name of the state, nation, race, you cannot sacrifice them. It is impossible to seduce them for any sacrifice. Real people are always for their own happiness. Their happiness is ultimate; they are not ready to sacrifice it for anything else. That's the problem.

So the society distracts every child, it teaches the child to be somebody else. By and by the child learns the ways of pretension, hypocrisy. One day—and this is the irony—the same society starts talking to you in this way, starts saying to you, "What has happened to you? Why are you not happy? Why do you look miserable? Why are you sad?" And then come the priests. First they corrupt you, they distract you from the path of happiness—because there is only one happiness possible, and that is to be yourself—then they come and say to you, "Why are you unhappy? Why are you miserable?" And then they teach you how to be happy. First they make you ill, and then they sell you medicines. It is a great conspiracy.

I have heard . . .

A little old Jewish lady sits down on a plane next to a big Norwegian. She keeps staring and staring at him. Finally she turns to him and says, "Pardon me, are you Jewish?"

He replies, "No."

A few minutes go by, and she looks at him again and asks, "You can tell me—you are Jewish, aren't you?"

He answers, "Definitely not."

She keeps studying him and says again, "I can tell you, you are Jewish."

In order to get her to stop annoying him the gentleman replies, "Okay, I'm Jewish."

She looks at him and shakes her head back and forth, and says, "You don't look it."

That's how things are. You ask me, "How can I be myself?" Just drop the pretensions, just drop this urge to be somebody else. Just drop this desire to look like Christ, Buddha, Mahavira, Krishna, to look like your neighbor. Drop competition and drop comparison and you will be yourself.

Comparison is the poison. You are always thinking in terms of how the other is doing. He has a big house and a big car, and you are miserable. He has a beautiful woman, and you are miserable. He is climbing up the staircase of power and politics, and you are miserable. Compare, and you will imitate. If you compare yourself with the rich people, you will start running in the same direction. If you compare yourself with the learned people, you will start accumulating knowledge. If you compare yourself with the so-called saints, you will start accumulating virtue and you will be imitative. And to be imitative is to miss the whole opportunity to be oneself.

Drop comparison. You are unique. Nobody else is like you; nobody else has ever been like you; nobody else is ever going to be like you. You are simply unique. And when I am saying you are unique, I am not saying you are better than others, remember. I am simply saying they are also unique. To be unique is an ordinary quality of every being. To be unique is not a comparison; to be unique is as natural as breathing. Everybody is breathing, and everybody is unique. While you are alive, you are unique. Only corpses are all alike; alive persons are unique. They are never similar, they cannot be.

Life never follows any repetitive course. Existence never repeats; it goes on singing a new song every day, it paints something new every day. Respect your uniqueness and drop comparison.

> To be imitative is to miss the whole opportunity to be oneself.

Comparison is the culprit. Once you compare, you are on the track. Don't compare with anybody—he is not you; you are not him. You are going to be yourself; he is going to be himself. Let him be, and you relax into your being. Start enjoying whatsoever you are. Delight in the moments that are available to you. Comparison brings future, comparison brings ambition, and comparison brings violence. You start fighting, struggling; you become hostile.

Life is not something like a commodity. Happiness is not something like a commodity, that if others have it, you cannot— "How can you have it, if others have happiness?" Happiness is not a commodity at all. You can have as much as you want. It simply depends on you. Nobody is competitive about it; nobody is a competitor to you. Just as the garden is beautiful—you can look and appreciate, somebody else can look and appreciate. Because somebody else is appreciating the garden and saying it is beautiful, you are not hindered; that person is not exploiting you. The garden is not less because he has appreciated it; the garden is not less because he is enthralled by its beauty. In fact, the garden is more so because he has appreciated it, he has added a new dimension to it.

> Life is not something like a commodity.

People who are happy are, in fact, adding some quality to existence. Just by being happy, they are creating vibes of happiness. You can appreciate this world more and more, if more and more people are happy. Don't think in terms of competition. It is not that if they are happy, so how can you be happy; it is not that you have to jump on them and snatch happiness away, that you have to compete.

Remember, if people are unhappy, it will be very difficult for you to be happy. Happiness is available to everybody. Whosoever opens his heart, happiness is always available. This happiness I call godliness.

It is not that somebody has achieved. It is not like a political post—one person has become the president of a country, now everybody cannot become the president, true. But, if one person has become enlightened, that does not hinder anybody else from becoming enlightened; in fact, it helps. Because Buddha became enlightened, it has become easier for you to become enlightened. Because Christ became enlightened, it has become easier for you to become enlightened. Somebody has walked on the path; footprints are there, the person has left subtle hints for you. You can go more easily, in deeper confidence, with less hesitation. The whole earth can become enlightened; each single being can become enlightened. But everybody cannot become a president. A country has six hundred million people, only one person can become the president—of course it is a competitive thing. But all six hundred million people can become enlightened, that's not a problem.

All that is divine is noncompetitive. And your being is divine. So just sort it out. The society has muddled your head, it has taught you the competitive way of life. Religiousness is a noncompetitive way of life. Society is ambition; religiousness is non-ambitious. And when you are non-ambitious, only then can you be yourself. This is simple.

How is one to be happy?

IF YOU WANT TO BE HAPPY, YOU WILL BECOME UNHAPPY: the very wanting will create unhappiness. That's why people are unhappy. Everybody wants to be happy, and everybody becomes unhappy. Can't you see this? Have you ever met a person who does not want to be happy? If you have met such a person, you will find that he is happy. If you meet a person who says, "I don't want to be happy, I don't care a bit," then you will suddenly see that here is a person who is utterly happy.

People who want to be happy will be miserable in the same proportion. If they want this much to be happy, they will be that much unhappy—the proportion of unhappiness will be the same as their desire for happiness. What goes wrong? People come to me and ask: "Everybody in the world wants to be happy—but then why are so many people, almost everybody, unhappy?" That's why—because they want to be happy.

Happiness cannot be desired. You desire, and comes misery; desire brings misery. Happiness is a state of no-desire; happiness is a state of great understanding that desire brings misery.

There are two ways to be happy—one is to snatch at life, the other is to let it be. The first demands happiness, refusing all else, and so lives between hope and fear, dream and rejection. The second way takes happiness when it happens but does not demand it, and accepts all else too. It is in the acceptance of all else that happiness comes; one is no longer bound by the fearful wish to have nor by the frantic will to hold nor by the fever to clutch at straws of certainty. There is instead the ease of swimming with the river where the river flows.

You ask: "How is one to be happy?" That means you want to snatch at life, you want to be aggressive upon life. You cannot be happy that way; life comes only to those who are not aggressive; life comes only to those who are in a deep, passive receptivity. You cannot be violent with life. Because you are violent, you are unhappy and miserable, you go on missing life, life eludes you. It goes on escaping from your hands. You are a rapist, you want to rape life—that's why you are miserable.

Life comes dancing, but only when you are not violent, aggressive. When you are not ambitious, when you are not even looking for happiness, when you are simply being here, suddenly you find happiness is showering—there is a meeting between you and happiness.

And one who really knows the art of being happy—that means non-desiring—knows also that whatever happens has to be accepted deeply, with no rejection. Then, by and by, everything is transformed into happiness. Small things that don't make much sense, when you accept them become very significant. Things that you go on rejecting create misery. When you drop your rejection and you accept wholeheartedly, you embrace them, suddenly you feel a grace arising in you. Slowly, slowly, as the understanding grows and as the desirelessness grows, one becomes overfull of happiness. Not only that one becomes happy, one starts overflowing. One starts reaching over to other people; one starts sharing one's happiness with other people.

So this is my suggestion: don't be aggressive, relax—that's how happiness comes. Wait prayerfully, gratefully—that's how happiness comes. Be receptive, be feminine, and happiness comes. Don't be male, aggressive.

You can see it around the world—countries that are too much after happiness are the most unhappy countries. For example, America is too much after happiness. That very hankering, that constant effort to be happy is making Americans neurotic. Almost three out of four are neurotic. And about the fourth I cannot say that he is not neurotic—he is also suspicious, ambiguous, vague. This has never happened in the history of man—so many people in a kind of neurosis, as if neurosis has become the normal state of humanity. It is because never before have people been so much after happiness, that's why.

Go to a primitive tribe, people who are still living without civilization, people who are called backward by Americans; just go, and you will find them immensely happy. They are backward, and sooner or later the missionaries will come and make them forward, will educate them and will open schools and hospitals and will do "great service" to them, and soon they will all be unhappy and they will need psychiatrists and psychoanalysts. Then the missionaries will be happy; they have done their job. How much they have served the people! They do great work, and they are really devoted people, but they don't know what exactly they are doing.

America needs to become a little backward—and those people who are backward, please leave them alone; they are the only hope. But we cannot tolerate those happy people. Maybe there is some jealousy—we cannot tolerate them.

Once a man came to me. For thirty years he had been educating aboriginal children in a jungle in Bastar; he had devoted his whole life. He came to Gandhi when he was thirty years old, and since then he had been working, he had devoted his whole life. He had come to me for help—he wanted some of my sannyasins to go and teach the aboriginals. I said, "You have come to the last man to come to—I cannot do such harm to people."

I know those Bastar people, I have been with them. They are

some of the most beautiful people in the world; they should be preserved. They are the only happy people—they still know how to dance and how to sing and how to love and how to enjoy life. They don't philosophize; they don't know arithmetic and they don't know history; they don't know geography and they cannot write. But they still have being; they still have grace. When they walk, you can see that they still have vigor; their eyes are so innocent. For centuries nobody has committed suicide; they don't know of anybody who has ever committed suicide in their tribe. And if sometimes murder has happened, then the person goes himself and reports to the court: "I have murdered. So whatever is the punishment, give it to me." He goes to the police station; maybe he has to walk two hundred miles because the police station is very far away from those jungles—and good that it is far away. The man who has murdered will walk two hundred miles and will go to the police station and surrender. Nobody was asking him, and nobody was after him. Beautiful people.

And they love immensely. You will be surprised—and they are called backward—they have a small hall in the center of the town, their village for their children. They have a small hall for their children; once the children are getting interested in sex, all the community's children sleep in that hall. They are allowed to make love, but nobody is allowed to move with any girl more than three days. So all the boys and all the girls become acquainted with all other boys and all other girls of the tribe. They learn nonpossessiveness, and love is just a play. And they are given all freedom— there are no taboos, there is no repression; there is no possibility. The moment a child becomes sexually capable or interested in sex, they are immediately moved to sleep in the common hall and they have to find partners. And they become acquainted—all the boys become acquainted with all the girls, all the girls become acquainted with all the boys. And only then they choose.

Once they get married, their marriage has an immense beauty. It is so intimate because it depends on a kind of attunement. The boy has been moving with all the girls, then he has chosen the girl who goes deepest into his heart, and with her he goes deepest into oblivion. He knows with whom he can have the greatest orgasm; now it is not guesswork. He does not decide by the size of the nose and the color of the hair—those are just stupid things—and he does not decide by the height and the weight. And he does not decide by clothes, because they are naked people. He simply decides by the innermost experience of orgasm—with whom he has the greatest experience, the greatest ecstasy. The decision comes out of that ecstasy. And these are backward people? These are the most liberated people.

And then naturally there is no divorce—there is no need because the man has found the woman, and the woman has found her man; they have found the right partner, as if they were made for each other. It is not poetic; it is not vague fantasy; it is not a head thing. It is a great experience, and once that experience has settled—and there is no hurry; the society leaves them alone, unless they decide, unless they find a partner with whom they really go into the other world, into the other dimension, with whom sex is no longer sex but becomes prayer—once they have found that partner, only then, even then, the society tells them to wait at least one or two years: go with the partner and wait two years after the decision before you get married. Because once you get married, then you have settled; then there should be no need. So two years . . . If the honeymoon continues and continues and continues, and after two years the boy is still going with the girl, and the girl is still going with the boy, and they both are still thinking of marriage, only then the society blesses them.

They don't know any divorce. Now, missionaries are very disturbed by these "ugly" people—they are ugly people because they allow sexual freedom. The sexually obsessed and repressed missionaries think these are immoral people. They are not immoral: they are amoral, certainly, but not immoral. They don't know any morality. They are more scientific, and their approach is more practical and pragmatic.

How do you decide? How do you decide that you are going to be with this woman for your whole life? The society does not allow you experimentation; you have not known other women, so you fall in love with one woman and immediately get married. Another day you see another woman passing by on the road— you are interested and you become fascinated. Now what to do? Jealousy arises.

Not a single illicit love affair is known in that small community of Bastar aboriginals. Once a person has settled with a partner, they have settled. There is no jealousy, there is no watching of each other; they don't become jealous of each other. They have settled out of their own heart experience; they have found their woman, their man. They don't know how to read—but what is there to read? They know how to read nature; they know how to talk to trees; they know how to have a dialogue with the sky. They know real reading because they read the book of life and nature. Yes, they will not accumulate much money: they will not become Fords and Andrew Carnegies and J.P. Morgans, they will not become so rich. There is no need for anybody to become so rich—because if a person becomes so rich, then millions of people become poor. Nobody is rich and nobody is poor. They have a beautiful tradition each year that whatever you have accumulated, you have to distribute; the first day of the year they distribute their things. So nobody accumulates much. How can you accumulate when each year you have to give everything away? All that you have, you have to distribute. So nobody becomes too attached to things; they are very nonpossessive people.

They have enough to enjoy; they work hard, they are healthy people, and nature supplies them more than is needed. If you don't want to become rich, nature has enough to satisfy you. If you want to become rich, there is no way for you ever to have contentment, ever to have happiness.

Somebody has asked a question: "Osho, you say that children should listen to the birds and not look at the blackboard. Then what will happen?" Then beautiful things will happen; then great things will happen. If for one hundred years all the universities are closed, and all the colleges and all the schools, people will become alive again. Yes, I know there will not be so much money to grab; money will disappear. But there will be more life—and that is what is needed. You cannot purchase life with money; you cannot purchase love with money. Money you have. The person who has asked this has also asked how they will earn their living—do you think that five thousand years ago when people were not educated they were not able to earn their bread and their butter? They were. Living was never a problem. And they had one thing more—life. Now you have only living, but no life; you think only of a better standard of living, you don't think of a better kind of life. You have quantity, but the quality has disappeared.

Nature is abundant; it is enough to fulfill us. But if our desires go neurotic, then naturally nature cannot fulfill those desires. When we are after neurotic desires—money, power, prestige— then naturally there is poverty, starvation, war. Wars and starvation and poverty exist because of your schools: your schools teach ambition; your schools teach people to be jealous of each other, to be competitive with each other.

What do we teach in our schools? For example, a teacher asks a question and the small boy cannot answer it. He may not have done his homework; maybe he fell asleep in the evening, maybe there was a beautiful film on the TV, or a thousand and one things were there to distract—and beautiful things, good things. Or there were guests in the home, and he enjoyed their company. He cannot answer. Now he is standing there like a culprit, a criminal, condemned. He cannot answer the question. And another boy is waving his hand and jumping and wants to answer it. Of course the teacher is happy, and the other boy answers it. Now, what has this boy done?—he has exploited the suffering of the first boy, he has proved himself better than the other, he has exploited the situation.

Now, this will not be so in a primitive aboriginal village; they don't exploit each other's situations. Anthropologists—who cannot understand this—have come across tribes who would not forgive this second boy because the second boy is cruel, violent. When the first was suffering, in a primitive society no boy would answer; they would all keep quiet. It would be thought ugly, violent, that when one is suffering, somebody exploits the situation and answers and enjoys. These people are thought to be backward? They are not; they are the only hope.

One thing more: the person has asked what will happen to people's lives if they don't know arithmetic and if they don't know geography and history. How will they earn their living? And what kind of a society will it be?

Yes, there will not be much money; there may not be big palaces; there may not be rich gadgets, technology. But there will be joy. And all the technology is not worth a single moment's joy. There will be love and dance and song and feeling, and people will again become part of nature. They will not be fighting with nature, struggling with nature; they will not be destroying nature. There will be no ecological problem. If schools continue, nature is going to die, and with nature we are going to die.

And one thing more: I am not saying that all the boys would like and all the girls would like to listen to the song of the bird at the window. No, there will be boys and girls who would like the blackboard more, who would like arithmetic more. Then it is for them! All do not need to be educated; that is my approach—only those who have an intrinsic feeling for it should be educated. And there are a few people who love arithmetic more than they love nature. There are people who love literature more than they love trees. There are people who love engineering, technology, more than they love music, dance, song. These are the people to be educated. All are not alike. These people should be educated as far as they want; they should be helped.

There should be no universal education: that is a crime. That means you are forcing people who don't want to be educated. That is undemocratic. Universal education is dictatorial.

In a really democratic world, a boy or a girl who wants to be educated will be educated. But a boy who wants to go to the carpenters will go to the carpenters, and a boy who wants to become a fisherman will become a fisherman. A woman who wants to cook will cook, and a woman who wants to dance will dance, and a woman who wants to become a scientist, a Madame Curie, will be welcomed.

People should move according to their inner nature; nothing should be imposed on them. This universal education is destroying people. It is as if—just think of another example—a dictator comes who loves dancing and forces everybody to dance. That would be an ugly thing. There would be people who don't want to dance, and if you force them to dance, what kind of dance would it be? If a dictator comes who wants everybody to become a poet, and opens schools and colleges to teach poetry and everybody has to compose poetry, what kind of world would that be?—a very ugly world. Only a few people—a Shakespeare, a Kalidas, a Milton, a Dante—would enjoy it. But what about others?—they would simply be miserable.

And that is what is happening. When you force arithmetic on

all, that is what you are doing. When you force geography on all, that is what you are doing. When you force anything on all, that is what you are doing. Nothing should be forced; a child should be allowed to find his own way. And if he wants to be a cobbler, perfectly good; there is no need for him to become a president. A cobbler is beautiful if he enjoys his work, if he is happy with his work, if he has found his work. No universal education.

Missionaries are the most dangerous people. A world without missionaries will be a beautiful world. With them, it has become a hell.

You ask: "How is one to be happy?" Forget about happiness; happiness cannot be achieved directly. Rather, think of what you enjoy, what you most enjoy doing, and get absorbed into it. And happiness will come on its own. If you enjoy swimming, enjoy swimming; if you enjoy chopping wood, chop wood. Whatever you like, do it and get absorbed into it. And suddenly when you are absorbed, you will find that climate coming to you, that sun-lit climate of happiness. Suddenly you find it is all around you. People have to get absorbed. Happiness is a by-product, it is not a goal. Doing the thing that you want to do, happiness comes.

Why do I always create misery around myself? I am beginning to see that I consistently choose this vicious circle. Is the choosing in itself the misery?

YES, THE CHOOSING IN ITSELF IS the fundamental misery. All other miseries arise out of it. The moment you choose, you are no longer whole; something has been rejected, something has been chosen. You have taken a side; you are for something, against something. You are no longer whole.

You say, "I choose meditation, and I am not going to be angry anymore"—misery is bound to happen. Meditation will not happen, only misery will happen. In the name of meditation, now you will be miserable—and one can find beautiful names for one's misery.

Choosing itself is misery. To be choiceless is to be blissful. See it! See into it; see as deeply as possible into it, that choosing itself is misery. Even if you choose bliss, misery will be created. Don't choose at all, and then see what happens.

But it is very difficult not to choose. We have always been choosing; our whole life has been that of a chooser. We have believed that unless we choose, who is going to choose for us? Unless we decide, who is going to decide for us? Unless we fight, who is going to fight for us? We have believed in a very stupid notion: that existence is against us, that we have to fight, that we have to be constantly on guard against existence.

Existence is not against you. You are just a ripple in this ocean—you are not separate from existence. How can existence be against you? You are part of it. It is existence who has given birth to you—how can the mother be against the child? This is what I call the religious consciousness. To understand this point is to become religious. Then you need not be a Hindu or a Mohammedan or a Christian, but you will be religious. In fact, if you are a Hindu or a Christian or a Mohammedan, you cannot be religious; you have not understood at all the depth of the religious consciousness.

> Existence is not against you. You are just a ripple in this ocean—you are not separate from existence.

What is religious consciousness? Existence is our home; we belong to it, it belongs to us. So there is no need to be worried, and there is no need to fight for private ends and private goals. One can relax with it—in the sun, in the wind, in the rain. One can relax with it. The sun is part of us as we are part of the sun; and the trees are part of us as we are part of the trees. Just see that the whole existence is an interdependence, a tremendously complicated network, but everything is joined with everything else. Nothing is separate. Then what is the point of choosing? Then live whatsoever you are in your totality.

The problem arises because inside you will find polar opposites, and the logical mind asks, "How can you be both?" Somebody else has asked me: "Whenever I am in love, meditation is disturbed. Whenever I meditate, I start losing my interest in love. So what to do? What to choose?" The idea of choice arises because there are polarities. Yes, it is true: if you go into love, you will tend to forget about meditation, and if you go into meditation, you will lose interest in love. But still there is no need to choose. When you feel like moving into love, move into love—don't choose. When you feel like moving into meditation, move into meditation—don't choose. There is no need to choose.

The desire for both never arises together. That is something tremendously significant to be understood: the desire for both never arises together. It is impossible because love means the desire to be with somebody else; love means to be focused on the other. Meditation means to forget the other and be focused on oneself—now, both desires cannot arise together.

When you want to be with somebody else, that means you are tired of yourself—and when you want to be with yourself, that means you are tired of the other. It is a beautiful rhythm. Being with the other creates a deep desire in you to be alone. You can ask the lovers—all lovers sometimes feel that desire arising to be alone. But they are afraid, because they think it is going against love, and what will the woman say, or what will the man say? The other may feel offended. So they pretend, even though they want to be alone, to be left alone; they want their own space, but they pretend and they go on being together. That pretension is false; it is destructive of love, and it makes your relationship phony.

When you feel like being alone, with all respect, with all love, tell the other: "A great desire to be alone is arising in me, and I have to go into it—there is no question of choice. Please don't feel offended. It says nothing about you; it is simply my own inner rhythm." And this will help the other also to be authentic and true with you. Slowly, slowly, if you really love a person, the rhythms start falling into a togetherness—that is the miracle, the magic of love. If love has really happened between two persons, this outcome is absolute, this consequence is going to happen. They will start finding at the same times the desire arising to be together and the desire arising to be separate. They will become a rhythm: sometimes coming together and being together and dissolved into each other, forgetting all about themselves, and then sometimes arising to move apart from each other, withdrawing, separate, into their own spaces, becoming their own selves, becoming meditators.

Between meditation and love there is no choice; both have to be lived. Whatever is arising in you, whatsoever is the deepest longing in the moment, move with that longing.

You say: "Why do I always create misery around myself?" There must be some payoff in it. You must be getting something out of it; otherwise, why should one create misery? But sometimes misery can give you tremendous benefits. You may not be aware of the benefits, you may be unconscious of the benefits, so you go on thinking "Why do I go on creating misery?" and you are not aware that your misery is giving you something you want.

For example, whenever you are miserable, people are sympathetic toward you. If you are miserable, your wife comes and puts her hand on your head, massages your body, is very, very loving, does not nag you, does not create any trouble for you, does not ask for anything. When you are in misery, there are many benefits. Maybe it is just because you are afraid your wife is going to ask for a new car—the new year has come, and the new models are in the market. Now, to be miserable simply makes sense economically. Now you come home with a stomachache and with a headache, you come with a long face, and the woman cannot gather courage to talk about a new car because you are in such misery.

You have to look around. Children immediately start feeling stomachaches when the bus arrives in the morning and they have to go to school. And you know it! You know why the child has a stomachache. But the same is the case with you. It is not much different; it is the same—maybe a little more sophisticated, more cunning, more rationalized, but it is the same.

When people start failing in their lives, they create heart attacks, high blood pressure, and all kinds of things. They are rationalizations—what can you do? Have you watched it? Heart attacks and high blood pressure almost always start to come near the age of forty-two. Why near the age of forty-two? Suddenly a healthy person becomes a victim of a heart attack. Forty-two is the age when life comes to a certain conclusion about whether you have failed or succeeded, because beyond forty-two there is not much hope. If you have made money, you have made it—by the time forty-two arrives, you have made it, because the days of greatest energy and power are gone. Thirty-five is the peak. You can give seven more years; in fact, already for seven years you have been going downhill. But you have done everything that you could do, and now the age of forty-two has come, and suddenly you see that you have failed.

Now you need some rationalization; immediately a heart attack comes. That's a great boon, a blessing from existence. Now you can fall into bed, and you can say, "What can I do? The heart attack disturbed everything. When everything was going to be okay, when I was just going to succeed, make a name or money, this heart attack has come." Now the heart attack is a beautiful camouflage; now nobody can say that you are at fault, that you didn't work hard, that you are not intelligent enough. Nobody can say anything like that to you. Now people will feel sympathy for you; they will all be good to you, and they will say, "What can you do? It is fate."

Misery is chosen again and again because it gives you something. You have to see what it is giving you—only then can you drop it. Otherwise you cannot drop it. Unless you are ready to drop the benefits, you cannot drop it.

The warden of the Elite Detention Home was giving a reporter a tour of his new model prison.

"Son," said the warden, "this is the latest in prisons. If this is successful, all prisons will model themselves after this one."

"I notice you have beautiful tennis courts and swimming pools," commented the reporter.

"And wall-to-wall carpeting in each cell" added the warden. "But we don't call them cells any more—just units."

"Those are nice color television sets in each unit."

"That isn't all. We have a tremendous auditorium, and every week the greatest entertainers perform."

"I certainly like the mess hall with the scenic murals on the walls."

"You mean the dining salon. The prisoners order à la carte and the chef's food is exquisite."

"The most fascinating thing I noticed," remarked the reporter, "is that there are no bars, fences, and almost no guards."

"That is because no one wants to escape," smiled the warden.

"How do I get into this resort?" inquired the reporter.

If prisons are made so beautifully, then who would like to get out of them? And if you are not getting out of your prison, look again: there must be something—wall-to-wall carpets, color television, air-conditioning, beautiful paintings, no bars on the windows, nobody guarding you—giving you an absolute sense of freedom. Then why should you try to escape out of it? The reporter is right. He asks, "How do I get into this resort?" The question is not how to get out of it; the question is how to get into it.

Look again into your misery; don't condemn it from the very beginning. If you condemn it from the very beginning, you will not be able to watch, you will not be able to observe. In fact, don't even call it misery, because our words have connotations. When you call it misery, you have already condemned it, and when you condemn something, you are closed to it, you don't look at it. Don't call it misery. Call it xyz—it makes a difference. Call it x, whatsoever the situation is, be a little mathematical—call it x, and then go into it and see what it is, what its benefits are, what are the main reasons you go on creating it, why you cling to it. And you will be surprised: what you have been calling misery has many things in it that you love.

Unless you have seen this and recognized those things that you would like to have, you will not be able to change anything. Then there are two possibilities. One possibility is: you stop thinking of getting out of this misery—that is one possibility because the benefits are so great

> Look again into your misery; don't condemn it from the very beginning.

that you accept it. And accepting misery is a transformation. The second possibility is: seeing that your misery is created by you yourself, by your own unconscious desires, and those unconscious desires are stupid; seeing the whole stupidity of it, you no longer support it. It disappears of its own accord. These are the two possibilities: either your support disappears and the misery evaporates, or you simply accept it because you like all the things that it brings to you, you welcome it—and in that very welcome, again misery disappears.

These are the two aspects of the same coin. But understanding is needed—total understanding of your misery, and you are going to be transformed. Either you will drop everything out of that understanding, or you will accept everything. These are the two ways, the negative and the positive, for the transformation to happen.

Barney visited his cousin Delbert in Taxonia, a small town in the Midwest.

"I hate this town," Delbert confessed. "I hate it with a passion."

"For what reason?" asked Barney.

"The taxes. We pay more taxes than any other town," complained Delbert. "And I hate taxes."

"Taxes are necessary to run the government," argued Barney.

"There are too many taxes here. Have you noticed mostly one-story buildings in this town? That is because there is a tax on all stories above one floor."

"That's not so terrible," answered Barney.

"Furthermore, have you seen many houses with front lawns?"

"Very few, I admit."

"That is because there is a tax on lawns."

"What's that patch of green lawn down the block?"

"That is the town cemetery where they put the people who are taxed to death."

"If you hate this town so much, why don't you leave?"

"I don't want to pay the moving and transportation tax."

Just look into your misery: either you will find it worth keeping—then accept it, then accept it with totality—or you will not find it at all worth keeping. In that very finding, it drops.

In a worldly sense I am happy in every way. But still I am not happy and cannot figure out the reason for my unhappiness either. Please, guide me.

ONLY A PERSON WHO BECOMES HAPPY in every way in the worldly sense discovers for the first time that happiness has no substance. The unhappy person cannot know this. The unhappy person lives in the hope that if he can find worldly happiness, then everything will be alright. The hope within an unhappy person is very alive. In the eyes of an unhappy man there is always a flame of hope. Only in the eyes of the so-called happy does this flame of hope vanish. This is why I continuously say that only the happy person—happy in the so-called worldly sense—can start off on the religious quest.

When you have all the so-called happiness, and you are still not happy, only then it becomes clear that there can be no happiness in this world. Whatsoever you could collect on the outside, you have collected. Now you are in a situation where all illusions have been broken, where all the mirages of all dreams have been shattered; you have lifted the veil and seen there is nothing inside and there is no one inside, there is only emptiness. You will certainly be troubled.

When someone becomes contented in every way in the worldly sense, then he finds himself in difficulty. "What is the matter? Now there is nothing I want. I have everything—money, status, respect, family—I should be completely happy; this is what I wanted. Until now I have been unhappy because they were missing, but why am I unhappy now? Now I shouldn't be unhappy."

Your illusion has been broken. What you had thought were the causes of your unhappiness were not the real causes. You were thinking that if you had all these things, that you would then be happy. But now that you have them, and happiness has not come, you find your whole analysis of happiness was wrong. Something else was needed in order to attain happiness. To attain happiness something must awaken inside.

Happiness does not come from the fulfillment of any outer conditions. Happiness is the shadow of the awakening of the self. Happiness is attained only by meeting the divine, and the divine is sitting hidden inside of you. But you go on running outside; you have turned your back toward it. Even if you go in search of the divine, you go outside—to Kashi, to Kaaba, to Kailash. You seek the divine in temples, mosques, and in gurdwaras . . . When will you close your eyes? When will you look within yourself? When will you seek inside the seeker himself?

Make a little contact with the consciousness that is within you. Spread your roots in it a little. Become acquainted with it. It is in this very meeting that happiness is born.

There is no happiness in the world nor can there be. There never was and there never will be. Happiness only happens when your meeting with the hidden inner master takes place.

Become acquainted with the divine, create a relationship with it, a love relationship, be joined with it by the thread of love—even a delicate thread of love and an infinite shower of happiness takes place. What you cannot attain in gaining the whole world is attained in a moment of enlightenment.

> Happiness does not come from the fulfillment of any outer conditions.

Wealth is inside. You have come with this wealth. Happiness is your nature. Happiness does not have to be acquired, and no condition has to be fulfilled. Happiness is unconditional because it is your self-nature. To be unhappy is unnatural; to be happy is a natural state.

Just as it is the self-nature of fire to be hot, it is the self-nature of man to be blissful. On seeing a blissful person don't think that something special has happened to him. The blissful man is the normal, ordinary man, the simple man. But when you see an unhappy person then know that something has gone wrong and this is something special. The unhappy man is not an ordinary man, because he has managed to demonstrate what should not happen. The happy man is exhibiting only what is meant to be, just as you don't call a cuckoo's cooing and singing something special. Yes, if one day a cuckoo should start caw-cawing like a crow, then there would be a problem.

Man's happiness is a completely natural thing. Just as the trees are green and there is a fragrance in the flowers and birds spread their wings and fly into the sky, in the same way happiness is man's intrinsic nature. We have called this intrinsic nature *sat-chit-anand*: truth-consciousness-bliss. It has three characteristics: truth, consciousness, and bliss. Truth means that which is and will never be destroyed, that which is eternal. Consciousness means awareness, wakefulness, meditation, enlightenment. And bliss is the culmination: the fragrance of bliss which arises in the person who is absorbed in meditation.

First become real so that you can become consciousness, and the day you become consciousness will be the day the fragrance of bliss will arise. The tree of truth bears the flowers of consciousness, and the fragrance of bliss is released.

Happiness has nothing to do with what you have or don't have. Happiness is related to what you are. However many things you may collect, perhaps they may increase your worries, your troubles, but happiness will not increase because of them. Certainly unhappiness will increase with them, but they have no relation to an increase in your happiness.

I am not saying that you should renounce things, that you should escape from your home and renounce the marketplace.

No, don't misunderstand my statement. What is, is good. Nothing will happen either by dropping things and escaping from them or by clinging to them. Remain where you are, but begin the search within. Much outer searching has already been done; now go within. Now know the one; in this knowing one attains all. All desires are at once fulfilled.

I so often come to the point where there is no more sense, worth, and meaning in my life. Everything that I start to do leads me to this point. And the rivers and oceans that I know are rivers and oceans of illusions, dreams, and fantasies, having nothing to do with Tao. Please, would you help me to understand all these illusory circles?

LIFE LIVED UNCONSCIOUSLY cannot have any meaning. In fact, life has no meaning in itself. Meaning arises when consciousness arises in you; then life reflects your consciousness, then life becomes a mirror, then life echoes your song, your celebration, your inner music. Hearing those echoes you start feeling significance, meaning, worth.

Living an unconscious life, you can go on changing from one work to another; it is not going to help. Maybe for a few days when the work is new and there is excitement, you may feel good. You may again project your illusions; you may again start expecting: "This time it is going to happen. Maybe it has not happened up to now, but this time it is going to happen." Again you will be frustrated. Every expectation is bound to bring frustration.

A man of consciousness lives without expectations, hence he

cannot feel any frustration ever. Sooner or later, when the honeymoon is over, you will feel frustrated. How long can the honeymoon go on? And each time the frustration is going to be bigger because your failures are piling up; it is becoming a mountain. And you have failed so many times that deep down somewhere the lurking fear is always there—even while you are on a honeymoon, deep down the fear is there that it is not going to be very different. You hope against hope. You have to hope in order to live; otherwise you will have to commit suicide.

So people go on changing their jobs, they go on changing their hobbies, they go on changing their wives, their husbands; they go on changing their religions. They go on changing whatsoever they can change—with the hope that this time something is going to happen. But unless *you* change, nothing is going to happen. It is not a question of changing something on the outside—you remain the same!

I have heard about a man who got married eight times, and he was puzzled: each time after four, five, six months, he will discover that, of course, the body is different, but the woman he has found is exactly the same as the one before—the same type of woman. He could not believe what is happening. He will change again; he will look for another woman with a different nose, with a different color, with a different hairstyle, maybe from a different race, a different country, but ultimately he will discover that only the outer layers are different, but the inner structure of the psyche of the woman is the same.

Unless you become conscious why you do a certain thing, why you choose a certain person, certain work, certain job, certain woman, certain man, you are bound to remain frustrated. Again and again you will miss the meaning of life.

Life is just an empty canvas; you have to paint the meaning on it. Whatsoever you paint will be the meaning of it.

So the first thing that I would like to tell you is: now rather than changing things—any outer direction, dimension—change your consciousness. The change has to be inner; only inner change can change something. Otherwise all changes are false, pseudo; it appears that something is changing, but nothing ever changes. Become conscious.

You say: "The rivers and oceans that I know are rivers and oceans of illusions, dreams and fantasies, having nothing to do with Tao."

No, you don't know. You have heard it, and you may have believed it. I am telling you every day that you are living in illusions. Listening to me again and again, you will start believing me; that is not going to help. This is not your awareness that you are living in illusions, dreams, and fantasies. If this is your awareness, the change is immediate; then you will not ask the question at all.

> Life is just an empty canvas; you have to paint the meaning on it.

To know the false as the false is to know the real. They are two aspects of the same coin; they are not different. If you know the false as the false, in that very knowing you have known the real as the real. It is a simultaneous experience. If you can recognize the false, you must have recognized the real; otherwise how are you going to recognize the false?

A person who is dreaming cannot know that this is a dream. And if he says in his dreaming that this is a dream, that means simply a dream within a dream, nothing else. You can dream within dreams within dreams; but if you really know this is a dream, the dream will immediately evaporate, disappear. The question would not have arisen. The question arises because you are still clinging to expectations. Yes, you are ready to accept that the past expectations were false, but the expectations that are right now surrounding you, alluring you—are they false?

"A terrible thing happened to me last night!" says Mario to his friend.

"But wasn't yesterday your birthday?"

"Yes! When I arrived at my office yesterday morning, my secretary invited me to go with her to her house!"

"And do you call that terrible? She is beautiful!"

"Let me finish. At seven o'clock I was at her door with a bouquet of roses. She opened the door, dressed in a beautiful, low-cut dress . . ."

"And then? What happened then?" asks the friend eagerly.

"Well, she offered me a martini, put on some soft music, and then whispered, 'I have a surprise for you. Come to my bedroom in ten minutes!'"

"And what did you do?" asks the friend.

"Well, after ten minutes I went in—and there were all my colleagues singing, 'Happy Birthday to You!'"

"Well, that was not so terrible!"

"Oh yes? I would have liked you to be in my place . . . I was naked!"

People go on living in expectations, illusions. One illusion is shattered, and immediately they start living in another illusion. They never become really aware that whatsoever your mind projects is going to be illusory. Your mind can only create illusions. Your God is an illusion, your meditation is an illusion, your yoga is an illusion, your Tao is an illusion, because these are all your mind projections. These are like the horizon that looks so close that one can reach it just within an hour—but one never reaches the horizon. It only appears; it does not exist. If you run after it, you will be running for eternity and you will not find it.

An Arab once came across a man walking across the Sahara Desert, wearing only a bathing costume.

"How far is it to the sea?" asked the man.

"About five hundred miles to the north," said the Arab.

"Bugger me," said the man, "I will have to stay on the beach!"

If you go on living in the mind, you will have to live on the beach; you will never reach the ocean. It is not even five hundred miles—it does not exist; it is a mirage.

Don't repeat clichés; try to see the point. Don't believe; try to understand. Stop projecting your fantasies, dreams, expectations on life. Completely forget that. The whole effort has to be one and single, and that is how to be awake. If you are awake, then things will be different, totally different. And there will not be any need to find anything special, to find meaning; then in the small things of life there is meaning, there is great significance. Each pebble on the seashore becomes a diamond. Then there are sermons in every stone, and songs hidden in every rock, and scriptures everywhere, because the world is full overflowing with godliness.

You are thirsty for meaning for the simple reason that you are not looking at that which is—and you cannot look at that which is, because you are fast asleep. Wake up! Come out of your grave. Unconsciousness is your grave. And then you will know what life is and how beautiful it is and how blissful it is and what a benediction and a gift.

> I have no interest in anything. It all seems to be meaning-less. Nothing excites, provokes, or challenges me. There is no juice, no zest. I have felt like this all my life. Why should I do this or that when nothing fulfills me anyway? I am always trying to be joyful—pretending to feel, to be excited, interested, and alive. I am always trying to be courageous, to jump over some of my fears. But for what? I am tired, I feel that "I am not"—and even that I don't really feel. Osho, where am I?

You say, "I have not got any interest in anything. It all seems to be meaningless." Does it have to be meaningful? Why are you expecting it to be meaningful? That very expectation is creating trouble. There is no meaning. In fact, because there is no meaning, joy is possible. Because there is no meaning, playfulness is possible. Because there is no meaning, dance is possible.

Listen to the birds—do you think there is any meaning? There is no meaning. But why should there be? See the trees too, the flowers, the stars—is there any meaning? But why should there be?

Once Picasso was doing his painting. A friend came to see him. He watched for a while and then said, "But I don't see any meaning in the painting." Picasso took him into the garden, showed him a rosebush with beautiful flowers, and said, "Do you see any meaning in these roses? If the roses have no obligation to be meaningful, why should my paintings be meaningful? I am enjoying painting them. If somebody can enjoy seeing them, good; if nobody enjoys, that is their business. But I have enjoyed just doing my painting—splashing color—I have enjoyed!"

A distant call of the cuckoo, and do you see the beauty of it? But you never ask about the meaning, what she is saying. She's not saying anything. It is just glossolalia; she's just enjoying, an outburst of joy. Children running hither and thither, so excited; do you think there is any meaning? Do you think they have found a treasure? Do you think they have found diamonds? Nothing much, maybe just colored stones or a dead butterfly, or maybe they have collected a few old leaves, seashells on the beach—but they are so immensely blissful.

Blissfulness need not be rooted in meaningfulness. In fact, the very idea of meaning destroys bliss. Once you start looking for meaning you become a calculator, you become a mind. You lose your being. Then you will be in tremendous trouble because everything will only make you ask again.

For example, "Why did God create the world? What is the meaning?" Even if some fool can supply you the answer—and there have been very foolish theologians who have been supplying all kinds of answers because whenever there is a demand there is going to be supply. When fools ask, "foolosophers" answer. But any meaning that can be given, "God created the world because of this . . ." Hindus say he created the world because he was feeling lonely. Seems to be meaningful. You can understand it: when you are feeling lonely, you start doing something—reading the same newspaper that you have read thrice before or fixing the radio which is perfectly all right. You have to do something; otherwise you start feeling meaningless. So, God was feeling meaningless, lonely; he started creating the world. But the question is: Why only at a certain moment did he start creating the world? What had he been doing before?

> Blissfulness need not be rooted in meaningfulness.

Christians say he created the world exactly four thousand and four years before Jesus Christ. Of course, it must have been a Monday when he started; the week starts on Monday! But the question is: Four thousand and four years before Jesus Christ—that makes only six thousand years ago—and what had he been doing for the whole eternity? Just vegetating? And if he could manage for the whole eternity, he should have managed for six thousand years more because six thousand years are not much compared to eternity. Not even six moments.

And if he had to create a world, he had to create this world? Maybe he was feeling lonely, but why have so many people to suffer for that? Let him feel lonely; he can commit suicide. But why should so many people suffer? And how is he feeling now? Very great? Since then he has not been seen at all. They say since he created woman, he escaped, he renounced the world. Must have become afraid. That was his last creation. First he created man, then he created woman, and since then nothing has been known about him. Maybe doing some austerities because he has committed such a sin! He must be doing penance, fasting, standing on his head, yoga postures, somehow to get rid of the karma that he has done, creating the world. But can't he "uncreate" it? Can't he say, "Lo and behold! This is the end!" Just as he said in the beginning, "Let there be light!" and there was light. Can't he say, "Let there be darkness!" and there is darkness? Has he gone dumb? He must have been dumb from the very beginning; otherwise why should he create this world? Such misery, such suffering that everybody is trying to get rid of misery.

Even the questioner feels there is no juice, no zest. What kind of world has God created? No juice, no zest—he should have learned something from Zorba the Greek: a little zest, a little juice. He should have learned a little laughter before he created the world. He created with such seriousness. That is the only thing wrong with God—he is too serious.

You say, "I have not got any interest in anything." Neither have I. But I don't see that there is any problem; I am enjoying it. In fact, since I lost all interest in everything, I have been in immense joy. Now each moment is just a joke. Then the whole thing is so ridiculous, I can even joke about God without any fear because there is no problem. One thing is certain: if ever I meet God I am going to hit him hard on the head, "You son of a bitch, why did you create the world? And particularly, why did you create the man who asked this question? No zest, no juice, nothing excites him.'"

Nothing excites me either. Nothing provokes him; nothing provokes me either. Nothing challenges him; he is almost close to enlightenment! That's how one becomes enlightened. When there is nothing to do, what else? Then one thinks, "Let me be enlightened now. No zest, no juice, no excitement, no provocation, no challenge. Why not be enlightened now?" That's how it happened to me. One day, I saw that there was nothing else left, so I said, "It is good now. Everything is finished, all is done, so I can be enlightened, at ease." And since then I have remained enlightened because nothing has happened to change my idea.

Life is meaningless, but that's why it can be enjoyed. If you start asking for meaning, you are asking for trouble. Then, kissing your woman, first you will brood: "What is the meaning of kissing?" There is no meaning. There are many aboriginal tribes who have never kissed—they rub their noses. It looks foolish to you—kissing looks foolish to them. And my feeling is they are more hygienic, rubbing noses is more hygienic. Kissing each other's lips is really dangerous. And avoid French kisses absolutely! Exploring each other's mouth through your tongue— absolutely meaningless. You won't find anything, believe me!

Unnecessary trouble. You may get a few diseases; it is simply an exchange of many germs, millions of germs. I think they say one million germs are exchanged in a single kiss. If people have lived for centuries without kissing, why can't you? If there were any meaning, they would have discovered it. If you have lived without rubbing noses . . . if there were any meaning, you would have discovered it.

In fact, there is no meaning. Meaning is only a mind desire. What is the meaning of anything? If you start asking that, naturally you will lose all juice, all zest. When you wake up in the morning, ask the question, "Why should I get up? What is the meaning of it all? And I have been getting up every day for thirty, forty, sixty years—what is the point of it all?" Every day you get up and nothing happens—and again you have to go to bed. When you have to go to bed again, why not remain in it? You will lose all zest, all juice.

Ask of everything that you do: Why should I do it? What is the meaning of it? For twenty-four hours, do this, and naturally the only thing that will be left for you to do will be to commit suicide. But remember, you have to ask the same question again: Why? Why should I commit suicide? What is the meaning of it? That will save you!

If you ask stupid questions, you will destroy your own life. What I am trying to point out is that the whole question of meaning is stupid. Enjoy, love, sing, dance! There is no meaning, so why not enjoy? If there was meaning, that means there would have been some kind of mechanical life. Machines have meaning. The car has a meaning—it transports you from one place to another. The food has meaning, the house has meaning—it protects you from sun and rain—the clothes have meaning, but life has no meaning.

That's why life is freedom. Meaning will become a bondage, an imprisonment. Only machines have meaning; man cannot have meaning.

But that freedom—once you drop that nonsensical idea of meaning, you will feel immense freedom. And in that freedom there will be juice and zest.

You say, "I have felt like this all my life." So, enough! You have done enough; now try my way. You have tried your way; try my way. Forget all about meaning; start living meaninglessly. Do all kinds of meaningless things, and see what happens. You will immediately become alive, immensely alive, because life has no meaning. So the moment you drop meaning, mind disappears and life possesses you.

You say, "Why should I do this or that when nothing fulfills me anyway?" It is not that nothing fulfills you, it is your "why" that creates trouble and that has created trouble for millions of people. In fact, all the so-called religions have been doing this stupidity that you are doing. They go on asking why.

There is a beautiful story by Turgenev . . .

In a village there was a poor man who was thought to be an idiot. The whole village laughed at him. Even if he said something very serious, they laughed, they found something idiotic in it. It was a determined thing that that idiot could not say anything meaningful. The idiot was getting tired of it.

A mystic was passing by. The idiot went to the mystic, fell

at his feet, and said, "Save me! The whole village thinks I am an idiot! How can I get rid of this idea that surrounds me? And everybody goes on and on hammering the same idea on me."

The mystic said, "It is very simple. Do one thing: for seven days don't make any statement on your own, so nobody will say, 'This is idiotic.' Instead, start asking 'Why?' to others—whatsoever they say. Somebody says, 'Look, the rose flower is so beautiful.' Ask 'Why? Prove it! How can you prove that this rose flower is beautiful? What grounds have you got?' And that will make him feel foolish because nobody can prove it. Somebody says, 'Tonight is beautiful, the full moon . . .' Immediately ask—don't miss any opportunity—'Why? What grounds have you got?' For seven days, don't make any statement that anybody can ask you why. Simply wait for others to make a statement. And ask. Somebody says, 'Shakespeare is a great poet.' Ask 'Why? What grounds have you got? It is all nonsense that he has written, all meaningless, gibberish. I don't see any beauty, any poetry in it.'"

For seven days the idiot did the same thing. The whole village was very puzzled. He made everybody feel idiotic. Naturally, they all started thinking he had become wise. After seven days he came to the mystic immensely happy. He said, "It was a great trick. I was not thinking that much is going to happen out of it, but now the whole village worships me."

The mystic said, "Continue. They will worship you because there are things—in fact, anything that is really significant is meaningless."

In dictionaries, significance and meaning are synonymous,

but in existence they are not synonymous; they are antonyms. Meaning is of the mind, and significance is a natural phenomenon. It cannot be proved, it can only be felt—it is a heart thing. When you feel that the rose is beautiful, it is not a head thing, so you cannot prove it. When you say, "This woman is beautiful," you cannot prove it; "This man is beautiful," you cannot prove it. Because you cannot prove it, it is not of the mind; it is a feeling—your heart starts throbbing faster.

When your heart feels thrilled, it is a totally different dimension; it is the dimension of significance.

If you can drop your search for meaning, you will be immensely showered by a thousand and one significant experiences. But if you look for meaning, you will lose all significance and you will never find meaning.

Mind is the most impotent thing in the world. It can make machines, it can create technology, it can do much scientific work, but it cannot create poetry, it cannot create love, it cannot give you significance. Significance is not the work of the mind. For that a totally different center exists in you—the heart and the opening of the heart. When the heart opens, the whole of life is significant—but I will not say it is meaningful. Remember the difference. I don't teach you meaning, I teach you significance.

And you say, "I am always trying to be joyful . . ." That is the best way to kill joy forever! Trying to be joyful? You say, "I am pretending to feel." These are the surest poisons to kill all feeling. You say: "I am trying to be excited, interested, and alive." In the very effort you have accepted that you are dead, that you are not interested, that you are not excited, that you are not feeling, that you are only pretending.

Trying to be joyful simply means you know perfectly well that you are sad. Now, you may be able to deceive others—how can you deceive yourself? You are trying to be joyful. You know perfectly well that you are sad. And each time you try, you are emphasizing your sadness. Each time you try to feel, you are going farther away from feeling. Each time you try to be excited, it is bogus. And you are becoming hypnotized by your repetition of being interested and alive.

This is a very suicidal course that you have chosen. If you are sad, be sad. Nothing is wrong in being sad. Be really sad; enjoy it! Sadness has its own beauty; sadness has its own silence; sadness has its own depth. And if you can be really sad, sooner or later you will have to come out of it. But that will not be a pretension; you will simply come out of it.

> Trying to be joyful simply means you know perfectly well that you are sad.

In my childhood I used to love swimming, and my village river becomes very dangerous in the rainy season, it becomes flooded. It is a hilly river; so much water comes to it, it becomes almost oceanic. And it has a few dangerous spots where many people have died. Those few dangerous spots are whirlpools, and if you are caught in a whirlpool, it sucks you. It goes on sucking you deeper and deeper. Of course, you try to get out of it, and the whirlpool is powerful. You fight, but your energy is not enough. And by fighting you become exhausted, and the whirlpool kills you.

I found a small strategy, and that strategy was—everybody was surprised—that I would jump into the whirlpool and come out of it without any trouble. The strategy was not to fight with the whirlpool, to go with it. In fact, go faster than it sucks you so you are not tired, you are simply diving into it. And you are going so fast that there is no struggle between you and the whirlpool. And the whirlpool is bigger on the surface, then it becomes smaller and smaller and smaller. It is difficult to get out until it is very small. At the very end, rock bottom, it is so small you are simply out of it. You need not try to get out of it; you are simply out of it. I learned my art of let-go through those whirlpools. I am indebted to my river.

And then I tried that let-go in every situation of my life. If there was sadness I simply dived into it, and I was surprised to know that it works. If you dive deep into it, soon you are out of it—and refreshed, not tired, because you were not fighting with it. Because you were not pretending to be happy, there was no question of fighting. You accepted your sadness totally, full-heartedly. And when you totally accept something, in that very acceptance you have transformed its character.

Nobody accepts sadness, hence sadness remains sadness. Accept it and see. In that very acceptance you have transformed its quality. You have brought a new element into it, that of acceptance, which is extraordinary. And in accepting it you start seeing its beauties. It has a few beautiful aspects. No laughter can have as much depth as sadness. No joy can be so silent as sadness.

So why not enjoy those aspects of sadness which sadness makes available to you, rather than fighting with it, rather than pretending the opposite? And remember one fundamental law: "*Aes dhammo sanantano,*" Buddha says. It is the law of life that nothing remains the same for long. Just enjoy while there is sadness, and nothing remains the same for long. Heraclitus says, "You cannot step in the same river twice; the river is so fast-moving." Life is moving like a river. So why be worried? If sadness is there, enjoy it while it is there. And soon it will be gone. If you enjoy it to the very core, it will leave you re-freshed, rejuvenated—and then there will be joy. And that joy will be natural and spontaneous.

You say: "I am tired . . ." You are bound to be tired because you have been fighting. Relax, let go, and all tiredness will be gone.

You are using the wrong language. You are fighting with exis-tence rather than being part of it, rather than welcoming its gifts, whatsoever those gifts are. Sometimes it is sadness, sometimes it is joy, sometimes it is dark, sometimes it is light, sometimes it is winter, and sometimes it is summer. Enjoy all the seasons. All those seasons are needed; the sun is needed, the rain is needed, the wind is needed, the darkness is needed, the light is needed. In fact, everything that exists has its place in life. Use it and you will not feel tired, you will feel overfull of energy. You will feel a dance of energy within you.

But you will have to change your whole approach toward life.

Could you explain about the path of the heart and keeping balance, because when I am in the heart, sometimes I feel happy and sometimes sad. So I can't see very well how I can follow the path of the heart and be centered.

NOTHING IS WRONG IN IT. You should allow it. Both are good, so don't choose.

Choice comes from the head. The heart knows no choice. Sometimes it is happy and sometimes it is sad. Both are natural and part of a rhythm—like day and night, summer and winter. The heart goes on changing its rhythm. The sad part is a relaxation part—like night, dark. The happy part is excited like the day. Both are needed, and both are coming from the heart.

But the question about it is coming from the head—that you want to balance. That you would like to remain happy twenty-four hours is from the head. The heart knows no choice; it is choiceless. Whatsoever happens, happens. It is deep acceptability. The head never accepts. It has its own ideas about how things should be, how life should be. It has its ideals, utopias, hopes. Drop the question and follow the heart.

When sad, be sad. Be really sad . . . sink into sadness. What else can you do? Sadness is needed. It is very relaxing . . . a dark night that surrounds you. Fall asleep into it. Accept it, and you will see that the moment you accept sadness, it starts becoming beautiful. It is ugly because of rejection; it is not ugly in itself. Once you accept it, you will see how beautiful it is, how relaxing, how calm and quiet, how silent. It has something to give which happiness can never give.

Sadness gives depth.

Happiness gives height.

Sadness gives roots.

Happiness gives branches.

Happiness is like a tree going into the sky, and sadness is like the roots going down into the womb of the earth. But both are needed, and the higher a tree goes, the deeper it goes simultaneously. The bigger the tree, the bigger will be the roots. In fact, it is always in proportion. A tall tree will have lengthy roots in the same proportion into the earth. That's its balance.

You may not bring it. The balance that you bring is of no use. It is of no worth. It will be forced. Balance comes spontaneously; it is already there. In fact, when you are happy, you become so excited that it is tiring. Have you watched? The heart immediately moves then into the other direction, gives you a rest. You feel it as sadness. It is giving you a rest because you were getting too excited. It is medicinal, therapeutic. It is just as in the day you work hard and in the night you fall deeply asleep. In the morning you are fresh again. After sadness you will be fresh again to be excited.

So each happiness will be followed by a period of sadness, and each sadness will be followed by happiness again. In fact, there is nothing sad in sadness. The word has wrong connotations from the mind. So simply be sad when you are sad. Don't create any antagonism and say, "I would like to be happy." Who are you to like it or not? If sadness is happening, this is the fact. Accept it and be sad, be totally sad.

Just whatsoever is the fact—don't move in any fiction—remain with that. Don't try to do anything—just be—and the balance will arise on its own. It is nothing that you have to do. If you do something, you mismanage.

So, good. The question is very significant, but remember it is coming from the head, so don't bother about the head. Decide for one month to live by the heart, and try in every way just to be with the heart. Sometimes it gives you dark nights, enjoy. Dark nights have very beautiful stars. Don't just look at the darkness; find where the stars are.

For the last ten days I have felt tremendously happy as I never did before. Just being myself and accepting me as I am feels great. Sometimes this incredibly good feeling is disturbed by two thoughts. First, will this stay that way? Can I keep this feeling in the future? And second, why did I have to become so old before I reached this point? I cannot forget, and still I feel sorry for all those years that I did not live at all. Please explain how to get rid of these disturbances of my happiness.

THIS HAS BEEN ASKED BY A MAN who came just six months ago and was one of the most miserable persons I have ever come across. It has been a miracle! He has changed totally. Now I can say just the opposite: he is one of the happiest persons around here.

These two questions are natural because now he is going to leave; he will be going back home. The fear arises: will he be able to keep this happiness that has happened to him?—the future. And the second question: he feels sorry for all those years that he lived but did not really live, that he missed. He could have lived those years as happy as he is now—the past. These are the two dangers to be alert about. Whenever you become tremendously happy, immediately the mind starts spinning its web.

And there are two methods of the mind, because mind exists either with the past or with the future. It immediately says, "Look, you could have been so happy your whole life." Now the mind is distracting you; say to the mind, "What does it matter? Those twenty years or thirty years or fifty years are gone. Whether I lived them happily or unhappily, they are gone; it makes no difference." In the morning when you awake, what difference does it make that you dreamed a very sweet dream or that it was a nightmare? What difference does it make? When you awake in the morning, both were dreams. And the night is over, and you are no longer asleep.

When the mind says, "Look, you could have always been this happy," the mind is creating an absurd desire. You cannot go back. You cannot do anything about the past; the past is gone and gone forever, irreversibly gone. Just think—even if you had been happy all those fifty years, what difference does it make now? Whether happy or unhappy, it is just a memory. In fact, whether your past even existed or not, what difference does it make now?

Bertrand Russell has written somewhere that sometimes he starts brooding about whether the past really existed or whether he simply imagines that it existed. Were you a child really, or did you simply dream about being a child? How can you differentiate now? Both are in the memory; whether you dreamed about it or whether you really lived it, both are part of memory, and there is no way to differentiate. The past is in the memory—both real and unreal. And psychologists say that when people say anything about their past, don't trust them, because in their past many imaginations and dreams have melted and have become mixed.

Their past is not factual, and there is no way now because everything is contained only in the memory. Whether you were really living it or you had just dreamed it, both have been mixed and melted into each other.

The past is just memory. But the mind can create great trouble, and by creating that fuss, it will deprive you of the happiness that is available right now. Just say to the mind, "I am finished with the past, and I don't care a bit whether it was happy or unhappy. It is gone and gone forever. Now is the only moment."

If you don't listen to this trap, then the mind has another trap for you. It will say, "Okay, the past is gone, but the future, what about the future? At least you can manage the future; it has yet to happen, you can plan for it. And wouldn't you like this beautiful space in which you are now to be there forever and ever?" Again the desire will arise. Don't say yes to it, because again it will lead you away from the present. And happiness is always herenow.

Happiness is something that belongs to the present. Now say to the mind, "I am not worried about the future at all, because if I can be happy now, this moment, I can be happy forever— because the future never comes as future, it always comes as the present. And now I know the secret of being happy in the present, so why bother about the future? Tomorrow will not come as tomorrow, it will come as today. And I have the key to open the door. At least this moment I am happy, and I know how to be happy in this moment. All moments that will come will come always as this moment." Have you watched? There is no difference between one moment and another moment. Time is completely beyond discrimination. It is always pure now.

So beware. These are the two traps of the mind. Mind cannot live without misery, so it is trying to create misery so that it can disturb your peace. Then the mind will be perfectly happy. Once you start feeling sorry for your past—it does not matter for what you feel sorry—you start getting sad, depressed. And once you start getting too concerned about the future, you become full of desire, tense, worried whether you will be able to manage or not, whether you will be able to perform or not. Between these two rocks, the fragile moment of the present is crushed.

So you have to be very alert. When one is unhappy, one can remain without alertness; one has nothing to lose. When one is happy, one has to be very careful and cautious; now one has a treasure to lose. And it can be lost within a second, within a split second—one wrong step, and it can be lost. And these are the two directions in which you can lose your treasure.

> Happiness is something that belongs to the present.

A person who is poor, a beggar, need not be worried that he can be robbed; but a person who has treasures has to be very cautious. When Buddha walked so cautiously, why was he walking so cautiously? He had something, something tremendously fragile, which could be dropped in any moment of unawareness and could be lost.

There is a Zen story . . .

A king in Japan used to visit his capital every night. He became aware that a beggar was always sitting alert under his tree;

he never found him asleep. The king went at different times, but the beggar was alert the whole night, just sitting there, completely immobile, with his eyes open.

Out of curiosity, one night he asked the beggar, "What are you being so cautious for? What are you guarding? I can't see that you have anything that could be stolen or that anybody could cheat you. Why do you go on sitting like that and watching?"

The beggar laughed, and he said, "Sir, as far as I am concerned I would like to ask you the same question. Why so many guards? Why such an army around the palace? I don't see that you have anything to be guarded. I have never seen a bigger beggar than you. You are completely empty, I can see through and through you. I don't see any treasure there; about what are you creating so much fuss? As far as I am concerned, I have a treasure, and I have to be alert about it. A single moment of unconsciousness, and it can be lost." And the beggar said, "Look into my eyes because my treasure is hidden within me."

And it is said that the king looked into the eyes of the beggar, entered into his eyes, and was completely lost. It was a tremendously luminous space.

He became a disciple to this beggar. This beggar was a Zen master—and the king had been in search for many years, and he had been to many masters, but he could never feel the vibe of the unknown. With this beggar he could feel it almost crystallized in front of his eyes, he could touch it. Something divine had happened to this man.

So when you have a little treasure to guard, guard it. Now these two will be the thieves: the past and the future. Be alert.

Nothing else is needed, just alertness. Just shake yourself out of sleep. Whenever you start falling into the trap, give yourself a jerk and remember.

I would like to tell you one of the most beautiful parables that has been written down the centuries. Parables have almost disappeared from the world because those beautiful people—Jesus, Buddha, who created many parables—have disappeared. A parable is not an ordinary story; a parable is a device, a device to say something that cannot ordinarily be said, a device to hint at something which can be hinted at only very indirectly.

This parable is written in this age; a very rare man, Franz Kafka, has written it. He was really a rare man. He struggled hard not to write, because he said what he wanted to write could not be written. So he struggled hard, but he could not control the temptation to write, so he wrote. And he wrote in one of his diaries, "I am writing because it is difficult not to write and knowing well that it is difficult also to write. Seeing no way out of it, I am writing." And when he died, he left a will in the name of one of his friends to say, "Please burn everything that I have written—my diaries, my stories, my parables, my sketches, my notes. And burn them without reading them because this is the only way that I can get rid of that constant anxiety that I have been trying to say something which cannot be said. I could not resist, so I have written. Now this is the only way. I have written it because I could not control myself. I had to write knowing well that it could not be written, so now, without reading it, destroy, burn everything utterly. Nothing should be left." But the friend could not do it, and it is good that he did not.

This is one of Kafka's parables. Listen to it; meditate over it.

I gave an order for my horse to be brought from the stable. The servant did not understand me. I myself went to the stable, saddled my horse, and mounted. In the distance I heard a bugle call. I asked him what this meant. He knew nothing and had heard nothing.

At the gate he stopped me, asking, "Where are you riding to, Master?"

"I don't know," I said, "only away from here. Away from here, always away from here. Only by doing so can I reach my destination."

"And so you know your destination?" he asked.

"Yes," I answered. "Did not I say so? Away from here, that's my destination."

"You have no provisions with you," he said.

"I need none," I said. "The journey is so long that I must die of hunger if I don't get anything along the way. No provisions can save me because the journey is so long, I cannot carry enough provisions for it. No provisions can save me, for it is, fortunately, a truly immense journey."

Now this is the parable. "The destination," he says, "is away from here. Away from here is my destination." That's how the whole world is moving: away from here, away from now. You don't know where you are going; only one thing is certain—you are going away from here, away from now.

The parable says it is an immense journey. It is really endless because you can never reach away from here. How can you reach "away from here"? Wherever you will reach, it will be here. And again you will be trying to go away from here. There is no way to reach this destination. If away from here is the destination, then there is no way to reach it. And we are all escaping away from here.

Watch. Don't allow this parable to become your life. Ordinarily everybody is doing this—knowingly, unknowingly. Start moving into the here; start moving into the now. And then there is tremendous happiness, so much so that it starts overflowing. Not only do you delight in it, it starts overflowing, it starts becoming your climate. It becomes like a cloud around you, so whoever comes close to you becomes full of it. Even others will start partaking of it, participating in it.

And the more you have, the more you will be drowning into the herenow. Then a moment comes when you don't have any space left for yourself: only happiness exists; you disappear.

But be alert of two things: the past and the future. And now you have something to lose; you are fortunate because you have something to lose. And you have a tremendous responsibility not to lose it. The mind will go on trying its ways for a time. When you become so alert that the mind cannot penetrate you and cannot disturb and distract you, then by and by the mind starts dropping. One day it understands well that now there is no way with you, so it leaves you. Then it stops haunting you. That day will also come. As you could not believe before that this happiness was possible; you may not be able to believe what I am saying now. That day will also come when there will be no distraction.

Then again you will have to be even more alert because you will start crying, "Why did I waste so many years with distraction?" And then you will become again concerned with the future. Many times you will come to face this past and future in many, many different ways. It is like a person going to the peak of a hill. He moves round and round the hill, the path moves round and round, and many times he comes to the same view, to the same place. A little higher, but the same place, the same trees, the same sky. Again and again, many times before he reaches to the peak, he comes to the same point, a little higher of course, but the same point, again and again. Many times he will come again and again to this same distraction of past and future. This is just the beginning.

But one day, one reaches the peak, and when one reaches the peak, all becomes available simultaneously: the valley, the sky, the clouds, the height, the depth. Everything becomes available. That's what enlightenment is.

All About OSHO

Your Most Important Web Link
OSHO.com/AllAboutOSHO

This website is a comprehensive online portal to all things OSHO, including information about his books and meditation techniques, audio and video recordings of his talks, and searchable text archives of his talks in English and in Hindi. Here you can find apps for your phone or subscribe to a "no-thought for the day," pick a card or do a reading with the OSHO Zen Tarot. You can find out how to subscribe to a regular newsletter or sign up as a subscriber to OSHO Radio and OSHO TV. There's a shop where you can find music for the OSHO Active Meditations or meditative music just for listening.

This page is regularly updated to let you know about new book releases and what's new in the OSHO TIMES online newspaper. It is regularly refreshed with features and excerpts from Osho's talks that address the most common questions people have about Osho and his work or shed light on the most pressing social, political, and environmental issues of our time.

An entire section of this page is devoted to the OSHO Meditations, with frequent updates and helpful content for those experimenting with these methods. Another section covers the programs and facilities offered at the OSHO International Meditation Resort in Pune, India, where an in-depth experience of Osho's vision of a meditative lifestyle can be experienced.

OSHO International Online also offers an expanding program of online meditations, courses, groups, OSHO Meditative Therapies, individual sessions, and other learning opportunities—all developed to dive deeper into and to discover your own being.

To contact **OSHO INTERNATIONAL ONLINE:**
www.osho.com/oshointernational, oshointernational@osho-international.com

About the Author

Osho defies categorization. His thousands of talks cover everything from the individual quest for meaning to the most urgent social and political issues facing society today. Osho's books are not written, but are transcribed from audio and video recordings of his extemporaneous talks to international audiences. As he puts it, "So remember: whatever I am saying is not just for you . . . I am talking also for the future generations."

Osho has been described by the *Sunday Times* in London as one of the "1000 Makers of the 20th Century" and by American author Tom Robbins as "the most dangerous man since Jesus Christ." *Sunday Mid-Day* (India) has selected Osho as one of ten people—along with Gandhi, Nehru, and Buddha—who have changed the destiny of India. About his own work Osho has said that he is helping to create the conditions for the birth of a new kind of human being. He often characterizes this new human being as "Zorba the Buddha"—capable both of enjoying the earthy pleasures of a Zorba the Greek and the silent serenity of a Gautama the Buddha. Running like a thread through all aspects of

Osho's talks and meditations is a vision that encompasses both the timeless wisdom of all ages past and the highest potential of today's (and tomorrow's) science and technology.

Osho is known for his revolutionary contribution to the science of inner transformation, with an approach to meditation that acknowledges the accelerated pace of contemporary life. His unique OSHO Active Meditations are designed to first release the accumulated stresses of body and mind, so that it is then easier to take an experience of stillness and thought-free relaxation into daily life.

Two autobiographical works by the author are *Autobiography of a Spiritually Incorrect Mystic* (St. Martin's Press) and *Glimpses of a Golden Childhood*.